foundati GEOGRAPHY 2

DAVID ROSE

OXFORD
UNIVERSITY PRESS

Oxford University Press, Great Clarendon Street, Oxford OX2 6DP

Oxford New York
Athens Auckland Bangkok Bogotá Buenos Aires
Calcutta Cape Town Chennai Dar es Salaam
Delhi Florence Hong Kong Istanbul Karachi
Kuala Lumpur Madrid Melbourne Mexico City
Mumbai Nairobi Paris São Paulo Singapore
Taipei Tokyo Toronto Warsaw

and associated companies in
Berlin Ibadan

Oxford is a trade mark of Oxford University Press

ISBN 0 19 913395 6

For Andrew, Stuart, Laura, Katie, Rachel, and my wife Rosemary

Acknowledgements

The publisher and author would like to thank the following for permission to reproduce photographs and other copyright material:

p11 South American Pictures/T Morrison, p13 Professor King, p17 Panos Pictures, pp18, 19 Tony Waltham, p21 Planet Earth/A Mounter, p22 South American Pictures/ T Morrison (left), Hutchison Library, p23 South American Pictures/T Morrison, p24 Panos Pictures/R Cousins, p25 Still Pictures (top), South American Pictures/T Morrison p26 Professor King, p27 Hutchison Library, p28 South American Pictures/T Morrison (left), Professor King, p29 South American Pictures/B Leimbach (left), Corbis UK (top), J Allan Cash, p30 South American Pictures/T Morrison, p32 Hutchison Library/N Smith, p33 South American Pictures/B Leimbach, p34 Picturepoint, pp36, 37 Corbis UK, p38 Hutchison Library (top & bottom), J Allan Cash (centre), p40 Hutchison Library (top), South American Pictures/T Morrison, p42 Professor King, John Sims (top left), p44 Hutchison Library/P Rippon, p47 South American Pictures/T Morrison, p49 Still Pictures, p61 Planet Earth/ I Edmonds, pp62, 63 Hutchison Library/E Lawrie/E Parker, p68 Corbis UK, p69 Professor King, p73 Panos Pictures/S Sprague/M Cavrallo, South American Pictures/T Morrison (top centre), p76 Corbis UK (left), Still Pictures, p78 Telegraph Colour Library.

Front cover photograph of Fremont River Valley, Utah, USA, by Images Colour Library.

The Ordnance Survey map extract on p58 is reproduced with the permission of the Controller of Her Majesty's Stationery Office © Crown Copyright.

Artwork by Jeff Edwards, except as follows: Technical Graphics p31, p32, p54, p59; Stefan Chabluk p18 (Figures 2 and 3), p21; Oxford Illustrators p13, p63, p75; Hardlines p47 (bottom).

Every effort has been made to trace and contact copyright holders of material reproduced in this book. Any omissions will be rectified in subsequent printings if notice is given to the publisher.

Colour Origination by Colourwise Ltd.
Printed in Spain by Gráficas Estella, S.A

Contents

World Map

80° N
70° N
50° N
40° N
30° N
20° N
10° N
0°
10° S
20° S
30° S
40° S
50° S
60° S
170° W
160° W
150° W
140° W
130° W
120° W
110° W
100° W
90° W
80° W
70° W
60° W
50° W
40° W
30° W
20° W
10° W
0°
Tropic of Cancer
Equator
Tropic of Capricorn
GREENLAND
ICELAND
Alaska (USA)
CANADA
UNITED STATES OF AMERICA
MEXICO
Hawaiian Islands
BAHAMAS
CUBA
HAITI
DOM. REPUBLIC
ST. KITTS-NEVIS
ANTIGUA & BARBUDA
DOMINICA
BARBADOS
ST. VINCENT
GRENADA
TRINIDAD & TOBAGO
ST. LUCIA
JAMAICA
BELIZE
HONDURAS
GUATEMALA
EL SALVADOR
NICARAGUA
COSTA RICA
PANAMA
VENEZUELA
GUYANA
SURINAM
French Guiana
COLOMBIA
ECUADOR
PERU
BRAZIL
BOLIVIA
PARAGUAY
CHILE
URUGUAY
ARGENTINA
REPUBLIC OF IRELAND
UNITED KINGDOM
DENMAR
FRANCE
PORTUGAL
SPAIN
MONAC
MOROCCO
ALGERI
MAURITANIA
MALI
CAPE VERDE
SENEGAL
GAMBIA
GUINEA-BISSAU
SIERRA LEONE
LIBERIA
GUINEA
BURKINA
IVORY COAST
GHANA
CAMEROON
EQUATORIAL GUINEA
GABON
A: ALBANIA
AR: ARMENIA
AU: AUSTRIA
AZ: AZERBAIJAN
AN: ANDORRA
B: BELGIUM
BA: BAHRAIN
BE: BENIN
BH: BOSNIA-HERZEGOVINA
BU: BURUNDI
C: CROATIA
CZ: CZECH REPUBLIC
H: HUNGARY
IS: ISRAEL
L: LEBANON
LI: LITHUANIA
LU: LUXEMBOURG
K: KUWAIT
M: MACEDONIA
MO: MOLDOVA
N: NETHERLANDS
Q: QATAR
R: RWANDA
S: SLOVAKIA
SL: SLOVENIA
SW: SWITZERLAND
T: TOGO
U: UGANDA
UAE: UNITED ARAB EMIRATES
Y: YUGOSLAVIA
ZIM: ZIMBABWE

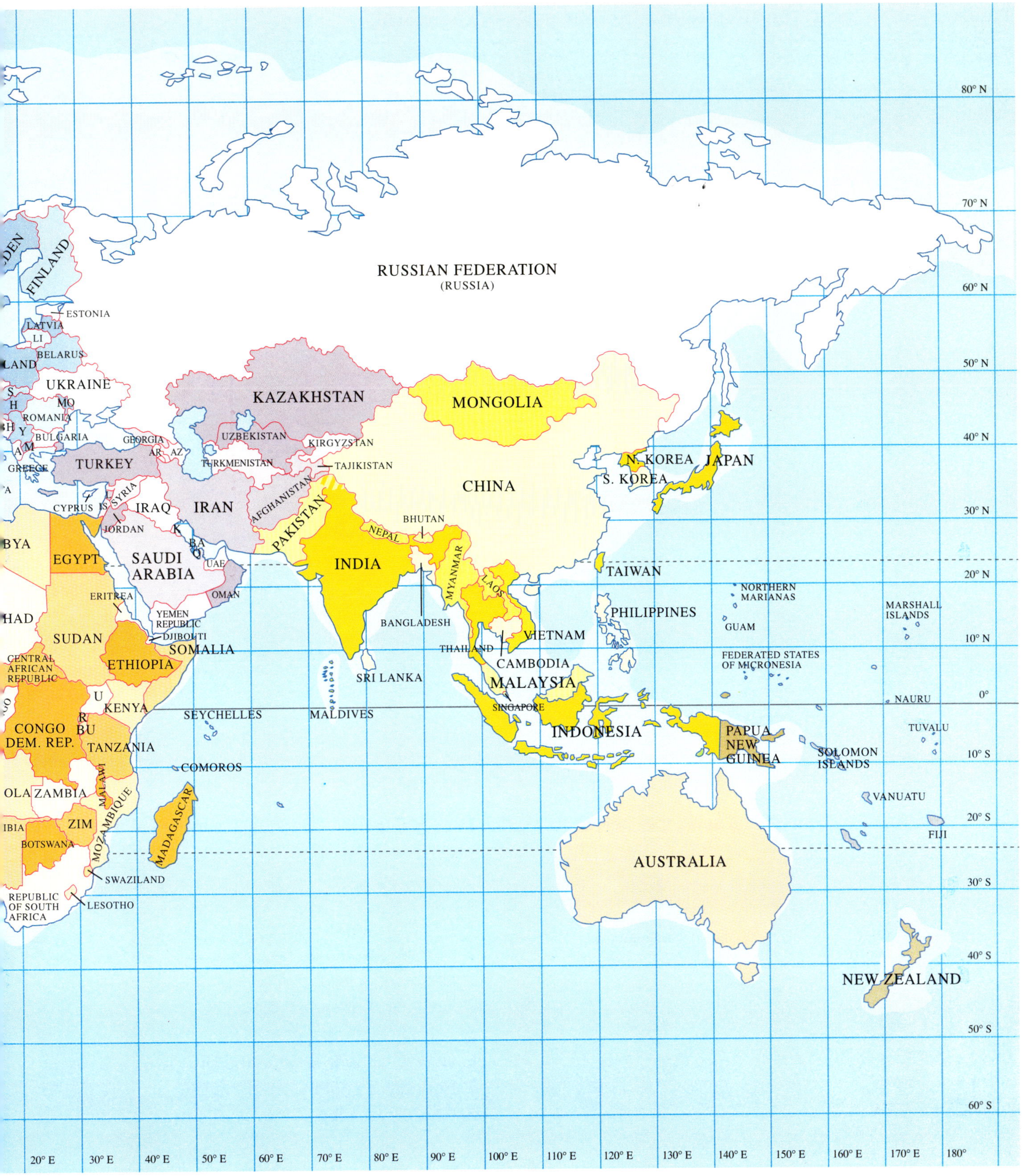
RUSSIAN FEDERATION
(RUSSIA)
FINLAND
ESTONIA
LATVIA
BELARUS
UKRAINE
ROMANIA
BULGARIA
GREECE
TURKEY
GEORGIA
KAZAKHSTAN
UZBEKISTAN
KIRGYZSTAN
TURKMENISTAN
TAJIKISTAN
MONGOLIA
N. KOREA
JAPAN
S. KOREA
CHINA
CYPRUS
SYRIA
IRAQ
IRAN
AFGHANISTAN
PAKISTAN
JORDAN
BHUTAN
NEPAL
EGYPT
SAUDI ARABIA
UAE
OMAN
INDIA
MYANMAR
LAOS
TAIWAN
ERITREA
YEMEN REPUBLIC
DJIBOUTI
SUDAN
ETHIOPIA
SOMALIA
BANGLADESH
THAILAND
VIETNAM
PHILIPPINES
CAMBODIA
CENTRAL AFRICAN REPUBLIC
SRI LANKA
MALAYSIA
SINGAPORE
KENYA
SEYCHELLES
MALDIVES
INDONESIA
CONGO DEM. REP.
TANZANIA
COMOROS
ZAMBIA
MALAWI
MOZAMBIQUE
MADAGASCAR
ZIM
BOTSWANA
SWAZILAND
REPUBLIC OF SOUTH AFRICA
LESOTHO
NORTHERN MARIANAS
GUAM
MARSHALL ISLANDS
FEDERATED STATES OF MICRONESIA
NAURU
PAPUA NEW GUINEA
SOLOMON ISLANDS
TUVALU
VANUATU
FIJI
AUSTRALIA
NEW ZEALAND
80° N
70° N
60° N
50° N
40° N
30° N
20° N
10° N
0°
10° S
20° S
30° S
40° S
50° S
60° S
20° E
30° E
40° E
50° E
60° E
70° E
80° E
90° E
100° E
110° E
120° E
130° E
140° E
150° E
160° E
170° E
180°

World Climates 1

- How well do you know Europe?

Let's use directions to find out.

This section is about the climate in different parts of the world.

The UK is part of Europe.
This map shows the countries in Western Europe.

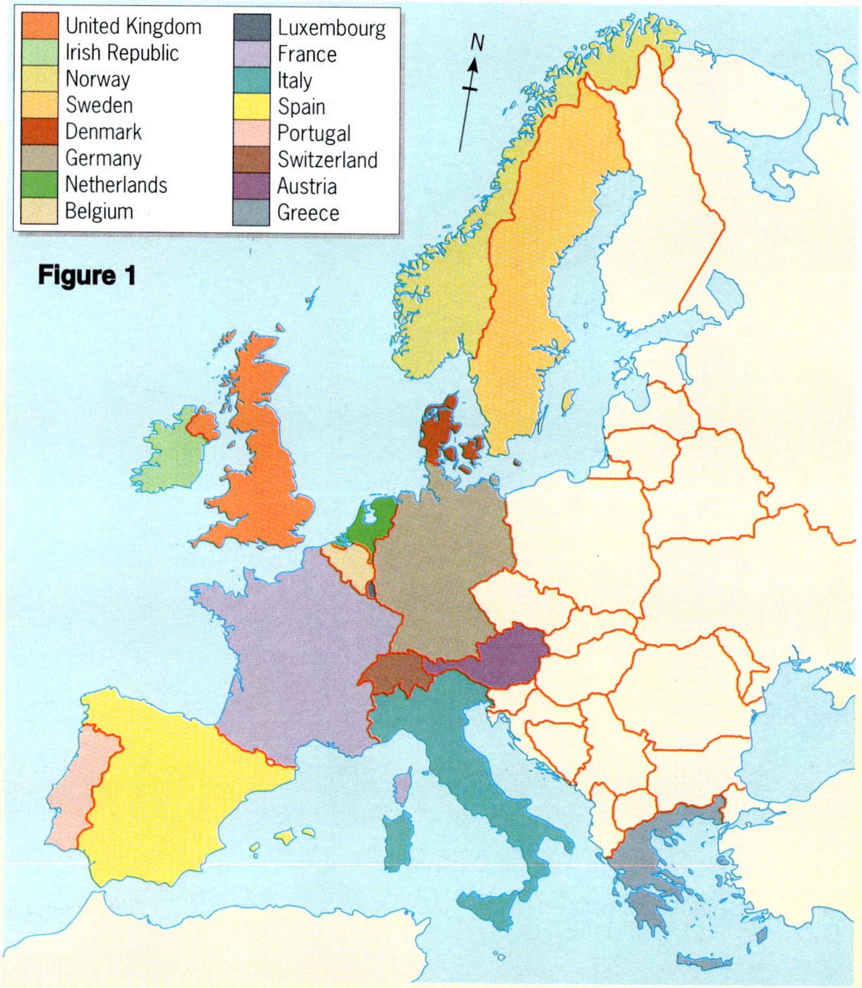

Figure 1

Activity A

Look at Figure 1 and name the countries shown by the shapes below.

Answer like this: 1 = **France.**

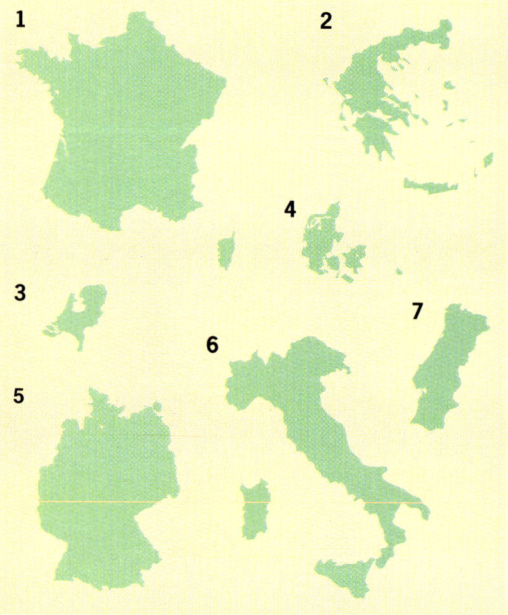

Activity B

Look at this diagram and finish the sentences below.

Answer like this:

1 The letter A is east of the UK.

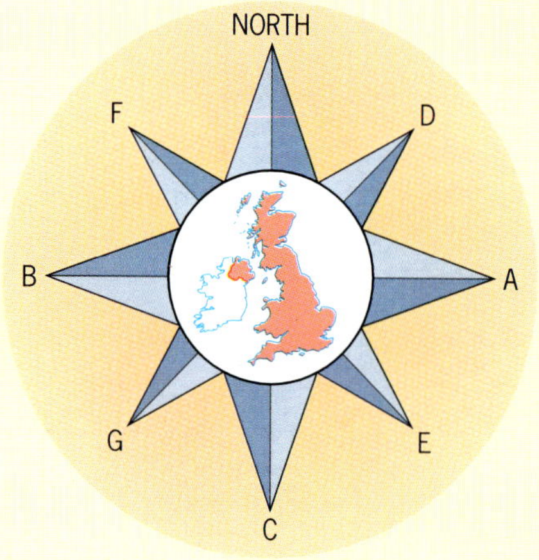

1 The letter A is ……
2 The letter B is ……
3 The letter C is ……
4 The letter D is ……
5 The letter E is ……
6 The letter F is ……
7 The letter G is ……

Activity C

Look at Figure 1. Read these sentences and then write **True** or **False**.

Answer like this: 1 **True**

1 Sweden is north-east of the UK.
2 France is south of the UK.
3 Denmark is west of the UK.
4 Spain is south-west of the UK.
5 Italy is south-east of the UK.
6 Norway is north-west of the UK.
7 Portugal is south-west of the UK.
8 Germany is east of the UK.

In summer, countries in the south of Europe are hot and dry. Many people from the UK go for a holiday to these countries, to enjoy the hot, dry weather. The countries of southern Europe include Spain, Portugal, Greece, Italy and parts of France. They are near to the Mediterranean Sea and so we say they have a **Mediterranean climate** (Figure 3).

In winter these countries are not as cold as the UK. They are mild and wet.

The summer temperatures in the UK are not as hot as they are in Mediterranean countries (Figure 2). But the winter temperatures of the UK are not as cold as they are in countries to the north like Norway and Sweden.

The temperatures in the UK are not very hot or very cold. They are **moderate**.

The UK has a **temperate climate**.

Figure 2 Summer temperatures in Western Europe

Activity D

Copy and complete these sentences.

1 The UK has a (temperature / temperate) climate.
2 Temperatures in Britain are (moderate / most).
3 The (north / south) of Europe is warmer in summer than the UK.
4 The (north / south) of Europe is colder in winter than the UK.
5 The south of Europe has a (Mediterranean / mild) climate.

Activity E

Look at Figure 2, and write down the temperatures in the countries below.

Answer like this: 1 England = 19°C, 20°C.

1 England =		**6** Norway =	
2 Italy =		**7** Denmark =	
3 Spain =		**8** France =	
4 Portugal =		**9** Germany =	
5 Scotland =		**10** Greece =	

Figure 3

Activity F

Look at Figure 3.

1 Name all the large islands on the map.
2 Name all the countries in Europe with a Mediterranean climate.

Activity G

Choose one country with a Mediterranean climate and write five sentences about its position in Europe.

World Climates 2

- Do you know the main places on a world map?

  Take a look at the map below.

This section tells you more about the world's climates.

On some maps a line is drawn around the middle of the Earth. This line is called the **equator**. The half of the world to the north of the equator is called the **northern hemisphere**. The **southern hemisphere** is south of the equator.

Most of the land is in the northern hemisphere. Most of the sea is in the southern hemisphere.

Some places are warm all year round. In the northern hemisphere these places are between the equator and the **Tropic of Cancer** (Figure 1). In the southern hemisphere they are between the equator and the **Tropic of Capricorn**.

The area between these lines on a map is called the **tropics**. In the tropics it is always warm because the sun's rays are strong all year round.

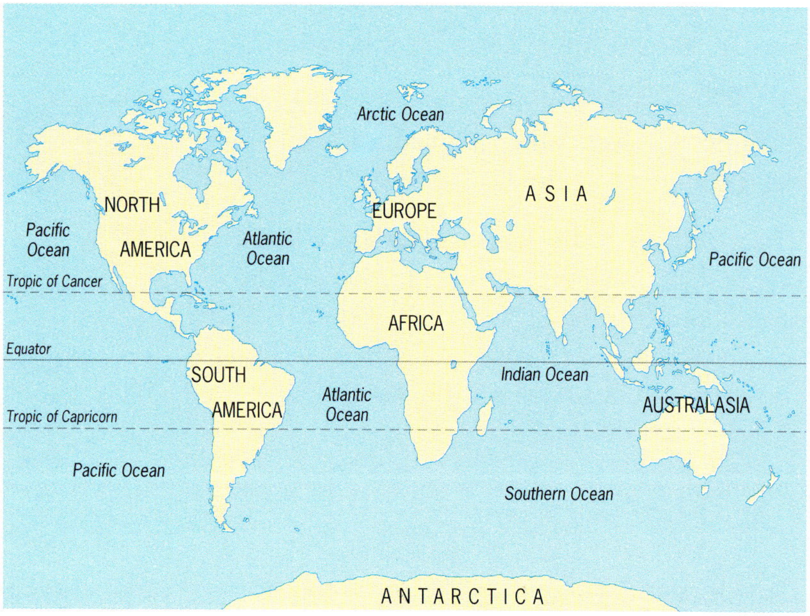

Figure 1 The world

Activity A

Copy and complete these sentences.

Answer like this: 1 **The UK is in the northern hemisphere.**

1 The UK is in the ______________ hemisphere.
2 Antarctica is in the ______________ hemisphere.
3 North America is in the ______________ hemisphere.
4 Europe is in the ______________ hemisphere.
5 Australia is in the ______________ hemisphere.

Activity B

Copy and complete these sentences.

1 The Atlantic Ocean is (west / east) of Africa.
2 The Indian Ocean is (west / east) of Australia.
3 The Pacific Ocean is (west / east) of Asia.
4 The Indian Ocean is (north / south) of Antarctica.
5 The Pacific Ocean is (west / east) of North America.

Activity C

Match these words with their meanings.

Capricorn	Cancer	Equator
The tropics	Hemisphere	

1 ______________ – the name of the tropic in the northern hemisphere.
2 ______________ – the name of the tropic in the southern hemisphere.
3 ______________ – the area between the tropics of Cancer and Capricorn.
4 ______________ – a line drawn around the centre of the world.
5 ______________ – one half of the world.

Activity D

Name three continents which are partly in the northern hemisphere and partly in the southern hemisphere.

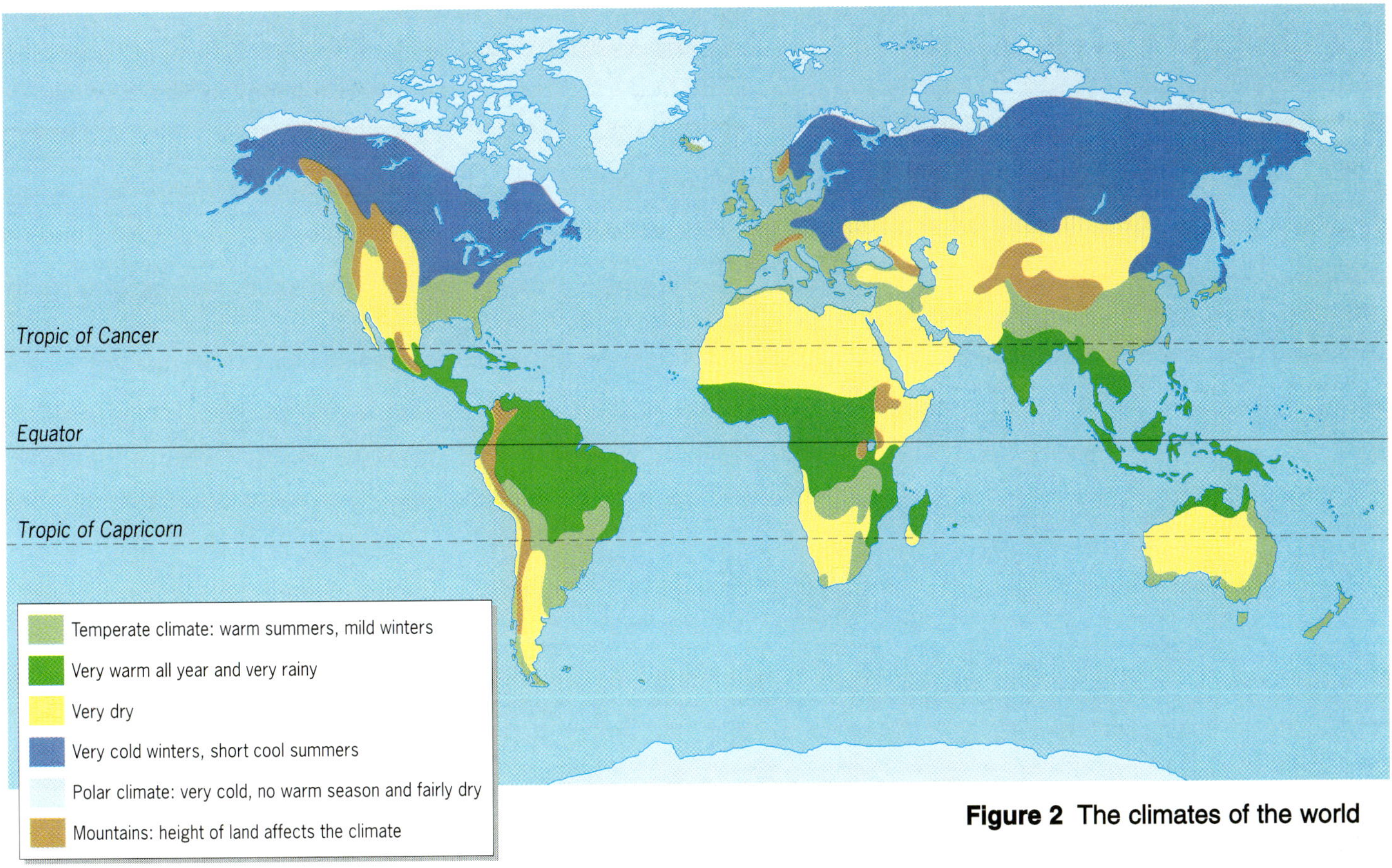

Figure 2 The climates of the world

Figure 2 shows the different climates in the world. The lines on the map make it look like a tidy jig-saw, but in the real world it is different. The change from one climate to another may take place over hundreds of miles.

One of the most important things to affect the climate of a country is the distance from the tropics. In the far north and the far south of the world it is very cold because the rays from the sun are not very strong.

The height of the land is also very important to the climate. It gets colder in the mountains.

Distance from the sea is also important. Where the land is near to the sea, the temperatures are lower in summer but warmer in winter. Also, if the winds blow from the sea they will bring rain.

Activity E

Name three things which will affect the climate of a country, and write a sentence about each one.

Activity F

Look at Figure 2, and list all the parts of the world that have a temperate climate.

Answer like this: South-east Australia, ...

Activity G

1 List all the climates found along the line of the equator.
2 List all the climates found along the line of the Tropic of Cancer.
3 List all the climates found along the line of the Tropic of Capricorn.

Activity H

Choose any continent and describe the climates found in that continent.

Ecosystems 1

- The world of nature is important to us.

Let's begin to find out why.

This section is about South America.

Figure 1 shows the countries of South America. Figure 2 shows some of the rivers and mountains of South America.

Figure 1

Figure 2

Activity A

Look at Figure 1 and list all the countries in South America.

Answer like this: South America = Venezuela, ...

Activity B

1 List all the countries next to Brazil.
2 List all the countries next to the sea.
3 List all the countries south of the equator.

Activity C

Name the capital city of each country.

Answer like this: Venezuela – Caracas

Activity D

Look at Figure 2.

1 Name three mountain areas in South America.
2 Name three rivers in South America.
3 Name three oceans around South America.

Activity E

Look at Figures 1 and 2.

1 Name five countries in the Andes Mountains.
2 Name a country along the Amazon River.
3 Name the rivers in Brazil.
4 Name the mountains in Brazil.
5 Name the biggest country in South America.

There are different kinds of plants in a warm climate than there are in a cold climate. Plants and trees are called **vegetation**. They are part of the **natural environment**. Figure 3 shows some of the natural environments in South America.

In the natural environment the animals and plants need each other to live. This means there is a **balance** between the animals, the plants, and the climate. An **ecosystem** is the name given to an area where there is a balance between the animals, the plants, and the climate.

But the natural environment can be changed by people. Towns, cities and farms take up the land. This means that the balance can be changed.

One of the most important ecosystems in the world is the **rain forest** of Brazil. But this ecosystem is changing.

Photograph 1 The rain forest

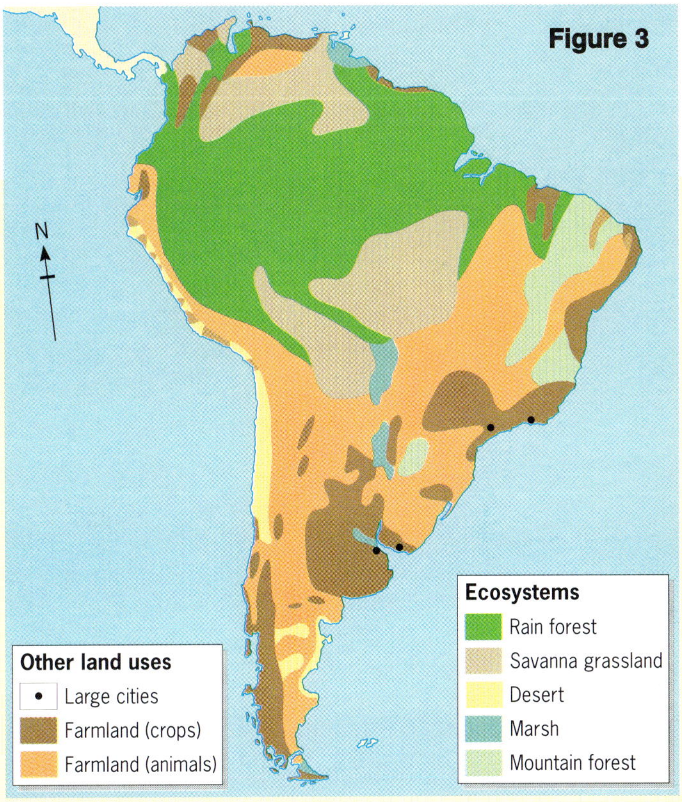

Activity F

Copy and complete these sentences.

1 The world around us is called our (environment / Earth).
2 Plants and trees are part of our (human / natural) environment.
3 Towns, cities and farms are part of our (human / natural) environment.
4 In nature there is a (balance / upset) between the animals, plants and climate.
5 Areas of the world where there is a balance in nature are called (ecosystems / environments).
6 One ecosystem in South America is the (rain forest / city).
7 The natural environment (can / cannot) be changed by people.

Activity G

Look at Figure 2 and Figure 3 and then copy and complete these sentences.

1 The selvas is an area of (rain forest / savanna).
2 The pampas is an area of (rain forest / savanna).
3 The Mato Grosso is farmland for (crops / animals).
4 The Atacama is an area of (marsh / desert).

Activity H

1 Name the ecosystems in Brazil.
2 Look at all the maps and write five sentences about Brazil.

Activity I

Why do you think people change the natural environment? Write down five reasons.

Ecosystems 2

- Some parts of the world have a long history.

  This has affected the natural environment in Italy.

This section is about Italy.

Look at Figure 1. The North of Italy is different to the South.

In the North of Italy, the summers are warm. But the South of Italy has a Mediterranean climate with very hot, dry summers.

The South of Italy is also called the 'Mezzogiorno' (Figure 2). It is a poor part of Italy. The soils are not very good for farming and there is little industry.

Figure 2

Figure 1 Italy

Activity A

1. Name the cities marked 1–10 on Figure 3.

   Answer like this: 1 = Palermo

2. Name the rivers A and B.
3. Name the seas C, D and E.

Activity B

1. Name the cities in the Mezzogiorno.
2. Name the cities in the North.
3. Name the cities on the coast.
4. Name the city in Sardinia.
5. Name the city in Sicily.

Figure 3

A very long time ago, the hills and mountains of Italy were covered in forest. But over many years the forest has been cut down. The slopes of the hills in the Mezzogiorno are now very bare. Plants and shrubs have taken the place of most of the forest. In the Mediterranean climate this type of vegetation is called **maquis**.

Like the rest of Europe, most of the natural environment in Italy has been changed by people.

The many farms, towns and cities mean that the balance of nature has been changed over many years.

Photograph 1
Bare slopes in the Mezzogiorno

Activity C

Copy and complete these sentences.

1 The cities in Italy are very (old / new).
2 The North and South of Italy are (different / the same).
3 The Mezzogiorno is the (South / North) of Italy.
4 The South of Italy is (richer / poorer) than the North.

Activity D

Look at Photograph 1. Write three sentences about the natural environment in the photograph.

Activity E

Write five sentences about Italy. The drawings below should help you.

Europe

- Do you know how to use the lines on a map to find places?

You will find out here.

This section is about the geography of Europe.

Figure 1
The countries of Europe, and their capital cities

Look at Figure 1. The lines going across the map on Figure 1 are called lines of **latitude**. The lines up and down the map are called lines of **longitude**.

Paris is at latitude 48N. Paris is at longitude 2E. So, Paris is located at 48N, 2E. Madrid is located at 41N, 3W.

The lines of latitude and longitude are measured in **degrees**, and the sign for degrees is °. So the line of latitude called 41 degrees north is written 41°N. The line of longitude called 3 degrees west is written 3°W, and so on. So Paris is really 48°N, 2°E. Madrid is really 41°N, 3°W.

Activity A

Name the cities located at these lines of latitude and longitude.

Answer like this: 1 59°N, 18°E = Stockholm.

1 59°N, 18°E
2 47°N, 7°E
3 60°N, 11°E
4 42°N, 12°E
5 38°N, 23°E
6 56°N, 12°E
7 49°N, 2°E
8 53°N, 6°W
9 39°N, 9°W
10 51°N, 0°

Activity B

Name the countries at these locations.

1 47°N, 3°E
2 42°N, 13°E
3 52°N, 13°E
4 51°N, 4°E
5 39°N, 4°W
6 38°N, 23°E

Figure 2 does not show cities or countries. It shows the location of the rivers, mountains, oceans and lakes. These make up the **physical geography** of Europe.

The highest mountains in Europe are in the south. They are the Alps.

The longest river in Europe is the Danube. It runs from west to east.

Across the north of Europe the land is flat. This area is called the North European Plain.

The English Channel is between Europe and the UK.

Figure 2
The physical geography of Europe

Activity C

1 Name five cities in Figure 1 not named in Activity A.
2 Give the latitude and longitude of the five cities.

Activity D

Look at Figure 2 and name the seas at these locations.

1 57°N, 3°E
2 40°N, 25°E
3 57°N, 18°E
4 43°N, 17°E
5 40°N, 5°E
6 43°N, 35°E

Activity E

Look at Figure 2 and answer the questions below.

Answer like this: 1 Tagus and Douro.

1 Name two rivers west of longitude 5°W.
2 Name two rivers east of longitude 20°E
3 Name three rivers north of latitude 50°N.
4 Name two rivers south of 45°N.

Activity F

Match these mountains with the locations below.

Alps	Pyrenees
Carpathians	Apennines

1 42°N, 1°E
2 46°N, 8°E
3 43°N, 13°E
4 48°N, 24°E

Activity G

Look at Figure 2.

1 Give the latitude and longitude of any five rivers.
2 Give the latitude and longitude of two lakes.
3 Give the latitude and longitude of two oceans.

Settlement in Italy

- How do we begin to find out where a place is?

Look in an atlas – like this ...

This section is about using an atlas to find places in Italy.

An atlas has two parts.
These are the maps and an **index**.

An index is a list of all the places shown by the maps. It is in alphabetical order, and is usually found at the back of the atlas.

Look at Figure 1. It shows part of a map index for the British Isles. Abercarn is at 51°N, 3°W. In an index it is written 51N 3W.

Figure 2 shows part of a map index for the world.

A

Abercarn, Gwent **13** 51N 3W
Aberdare, Mid Glamorgan **13** 51N 3W
Aberdeen, Grampian **16** 57N 2W
Abergavenny, Gwent **13** 51N 3W
Abergele, Clwyd **13** 53N 3W
Abertillery, Gwent **13** 51N 3W
Aberystwyth, Dyfed **13** 52N 4W
Abingdon, Oxfordshire **12** 51N 1W
Accrington, Lancashire **14** 53N 2W
Achill Island, Irish Republic **17** 54N 10W

Figure 1

Activity A

Look at Figure 1. Name the page where these places are located in the atlas.

Answer like this: 1 Abercarn – page 13.

1 Abercarn –
2 Accrington –
3 Aberdeen –
4 Abergavenny –
5 Abergele –
6 Achill Island –

Activity B

Look at Figure 2 and write down the latitude and longitude of these places.

Answer like this: 1 Padua – 45N 12E.

1 Padua –
2 Parma –
3 Paotow –
4 Palma –
5 Palm Beach –
6 Paraguay –
7 Palermo –
8 Paramaribo –

Activity C

Look at Figure 2 and name the countries where these places are located.

Answer like this: 1 Padua is in Italy.

1 Padua
2 Paotow
3 Parma
4 Palma
5 Palermo
6 Pampa

P

Padua, *Italy* **24** 45N 12E
Palermo, *Italy* **24** 38N 13E
Palma, *Spain* **24** 39N 2E
Palm Beach, *USA* **46** 26N 80W
Pampa, *Argentina* **49** 36S 62W
PANAMA, *Central America* **47** 9N 80W
Paotow, *China* **31** 40N 110E
PARAGUAY, *S.America* **52** 23S 58W
Paramaribo, *Surinam* **52** 5N 55W
Parma, *Italy* **24** 44N 10E

Figure 2

Activity D

Copy the names of these countries in alphabetical order.

1 Italy, Spain, France, Norway, Germany, Wales.
2 Colombia, Brazil, Paraguay, Surinam, Argentina.
3 Italy, Ireland, Bolivia, Brazil, China, Colombia.
4 Australia, Austria, Algeria, Albania, Argentina.
5 Ireland, Iran, Colombia, Chile, USA, UK.

Activity E

Use the index of an atlas and give the latitude and longitude of ten cities in the world.

The capital city of Italy is Rome. It is one of the oldest cities in the world. Many of the other cities in Italy are also very old.

Cities like Florence, Venice and Rome are very beautiful. Many **tourists** go to visit them every year.

Figure 1 shows where the Italian people live. The population of the UK is just under 57½ million. The population of Italy is just over 57½ million.

Photograph 1 Venice

Figure 3
Population map of Italy

Activity F

Look at Figure 3. Name the cities at these locations.

Answer like this: 1 42°N, 12°E – Rome.

1 42°N, 12°E –
2 38°N, 13°E –
3 45°N, 7°E –
4 45°N, 9°E –
5 44°N, 9°E –
6 41°N, 14°E –

Activity G

Look at Figure 3 and write down the latitude and longitude of these cities in Italy.

1 Venice
2 Cagliari
3 Bari
4 Pisa
5 Florence

Activity H

Look at Figure 3.

1 Write three sentences about the location of the areas where most people in Italy live.
2 Write three sentences about the location of the areas where few people in Italy live.
3 How many cities are there in Italy with more than half a million people?

Activity I

Look at the photograph of Venice. Write at least three sentences to explain why a tourist would like to visit it.

Activity J

Use an atlas to find these places in Italy.

1 Messina, Sassari, Parma, Padua, Bologna.
2 River Tiber, River Po, Lake Garda.

Volcanoes 1

- What exactly is a volcano?

Italy has two famous volcanoes.

This section is about volcanoes in Italy.

A volcano is a type of mountain. Look at Photograph 1. It shows Mount Vesuvius in Italy. Mount Vesuvius is a volcano.

Deep inside the Earth it is so hot that rock melts. Melted or molten rock is called **magma**. In some places the magma breaks through a crack in the Earth. The crack is called a **fault**. The very hot flowing rock is then called **lava**.

As the lava cools on the surface it turns to solid rock. The rock builds up near the fault to make a **volcano**.

When the lava breaks through the fault there is an **eruption**.

Figure 2 shows what it is like inside a volcano.

Photograph 1

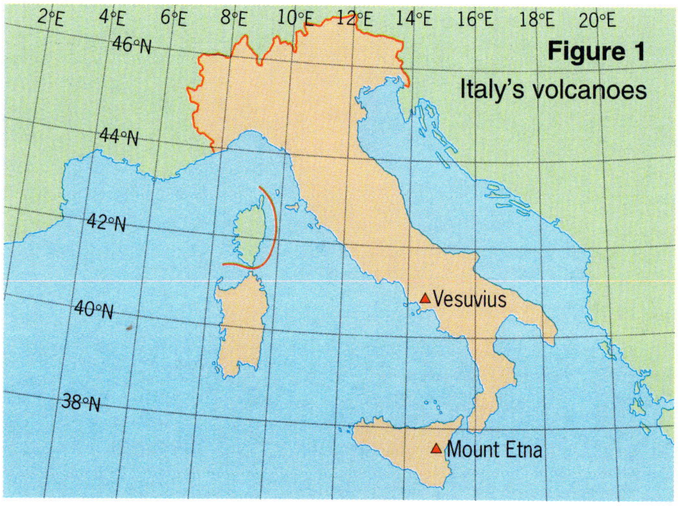

Figure 1
Italy's volcanoes

Activity A

Look at Figure 1 and name the volcanoes at these locations.

1 37°N, 15°E **2** 41°N, 14°E

Activity B

1 Match the letters on Figure 3 with the words below.

Answer like this: A = Magma

Crater	Magma	Vent
Lava	Steam cloud	Cone

2 Copy and label Figure 3.

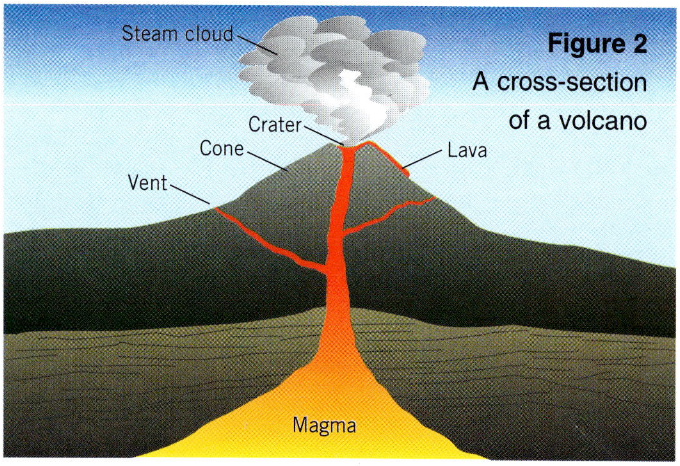

Figure 2
A cross-section of a volcano

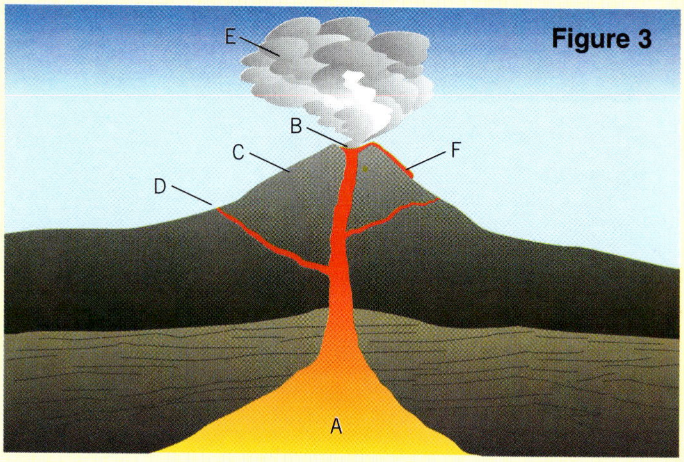

Figure 3

Italy has two large volcanoes. Figure 1 shows they are both in the Mezzogiorno, or South of Italy. The volcanoes are Mount Etna on the island of Sicily, and Mount Vesuvius near Naples.

A volcano that is likely to have an eruption is called an **active** volcano. If the volcano is dead and an eruption is not likely, the volcano is **extinct**. A sleeping volcano is said to be **dormant**.

Etna and Vesuvius are active volcanoes.

In the year 79 AD it was thought that Vesuvius was dormant, but there was a big eruption. Ash and mud from the eruption covered the settlements of Pompeii and Herculaneum. Many people were killed.

Photograph 2

Today, Etna is the largest active volcano in Europe. When there is an eruption, the lava flows down the sides of the volcano and destroys the farms on its slopes (Photograph 2).

All over the world the soils around volcanoes are usually very good for farming. This has been the main reason why people have always lived near volcanoes.

In Italy there are many farms around Etna and Vesuvius. There are **vineyards** where grapes are grown. The grapes are used to make wine.

Activity C

Copy and complete the sentences below using these words.

Answer like this: 1 A volcano is a type of mountain.

magma volcano fault lava eruption

1 A __________ is a type of mountain.
2 A big crack in the rock is called a __________ .
3 Rock that melts deep inside the earth is called __________ .
4 Rock that melts on the surface is called __________ .
5 Lava comes from a volcano when there is an __________ .

Activity D

Write three sentences to explain the differences between an extinct volcano, a dormant volcano and an active volcano.

Activity E

Match the words below with their meanings.

Vineyard	Mezzogiorno	Tourist
Sicily	Pompeii	Wine

– a person on holiday.
– an island in Italy.
– a farm that grows grapes.
– the south of Italy.
– a very old settlement near Vesuvius.
– a drink made from grapes.

Activity F

Look at Photograph 1 and Photograph 2.

1 Which photograph shows a steam cloud?
2 Which photograph shows the volcano when it is dormant?
3 Write three sentences about farming around Vesuvius or Etna.

Volcanoes 2

- Where are volcanoes, and do we have any in the UK?

Let's find out using maps.

This section is about volcanoes in the rest of the world.

Figure 1 shows the location of some of the largest volcanoes in the world. It also shows the parts of the world where there are earthquakes.

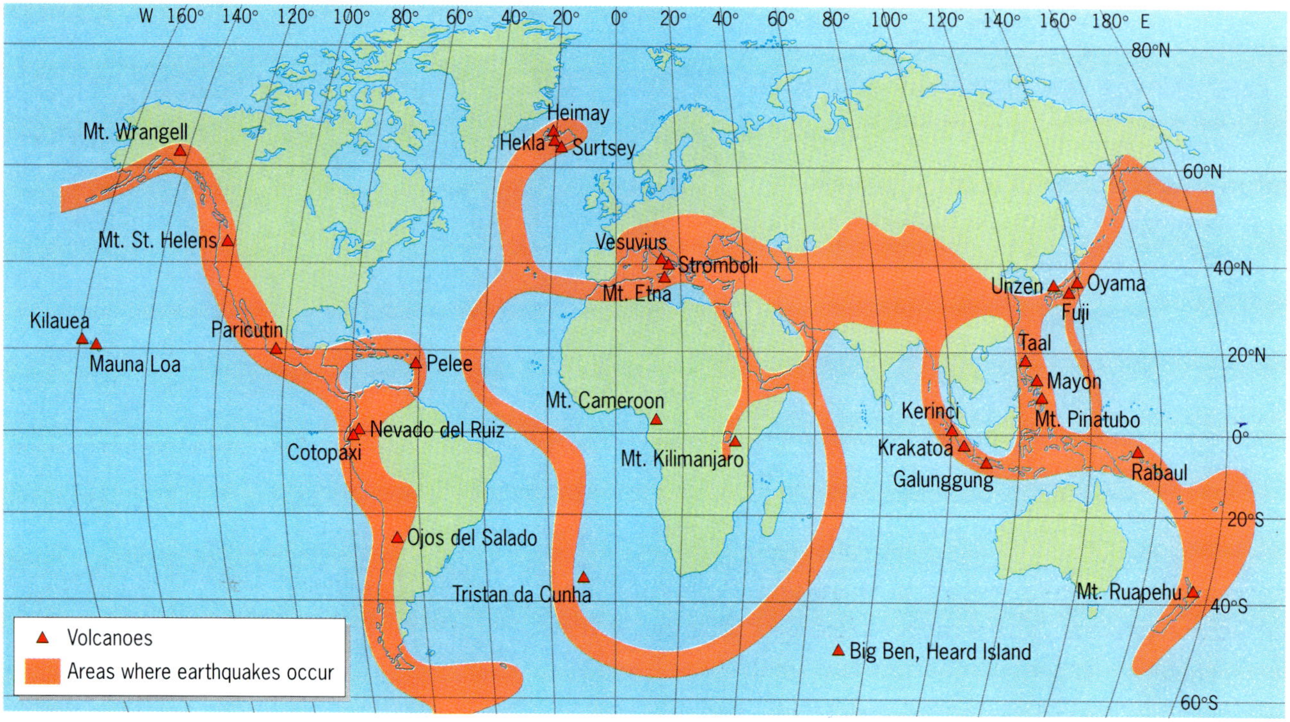

Figure 1

Activity A

Look at Figure 1.

1 Name a volcano in Europe.
2 Name a volcano in North America.
3 Name a volcano in South America.
4 Name a volcano in Asia.
5 Name a volcano in Africa.
6 Name a volcano in Italy.

Activity B

Look at Figure 1 and name all the volcanoes below.

Answer like this: 1 **37°N, 15°E – Mount Etna.**

1 37°N, 15°E	**6** 3°N, 11°E
2 6°S, 105°E	**7** 46°N, 122°W
3 35°N, 138°E	**8** 20°N, 155°W
4 63°N, 20°W	**9** 3°S, 37°E
5 19°N, 102°W	**10** 0°, 78°W

Activity C

1 Name five volcanoes in Figure 1 which are not named in Activity B.
2 Write down the latitude and longitude of the five volcanoes you have named.

Activity D

Write down if these places are in the earthquake areas.

Answer like this: 1 **40°N, 30°W – yes.**

1 40°N, 30°W	**5** 36°N, 138°E
2 20°S, 70°W	**6** 20°N, 10°W
3 20°S, 180°E	**7** 60°S, 80°E
4 40°N, 80°E	**8** 49°N, 123°W

Activity E

Use an atlas to name ten countries in the earthquake areas.

The world's volcanoes are all along the lines of faults in the Earth. This means they are at places where the Earth is weak. So there is likely to be some movement of the Earth.

This is why volcanoes and earthquakes are located together. An earthquake is a shaking of the land. Earthquakes are caused by movement deep inside the Earth.

Not all volcanoes are the same. A volcano's shape comes from the lava. If the lava flows quickly, the sides will be low. This makes a **shield volcano** (Figure 2).

If the lava flows slowly, the sides of the volcano will be steep. This makes a **cone volcano**.

Some volcanoes throw out ash, dust and gas when they erupt. These are called **ash** or **cinder volcanoes**.

Some volcanoes throw out lava and ash. These volcanoes are called **composite cone volcanoes**. Vesuvius and Etna are like this.

If the sides of a volcano are very steep, the soils can be washed away by the rain. In hot parts of the world this can happen very quickly as it rains hard and often. Farmers cut large steps into the side of the volcano to make flat areas. These steps are called **terraces**, and they stop the soil from being washed away.

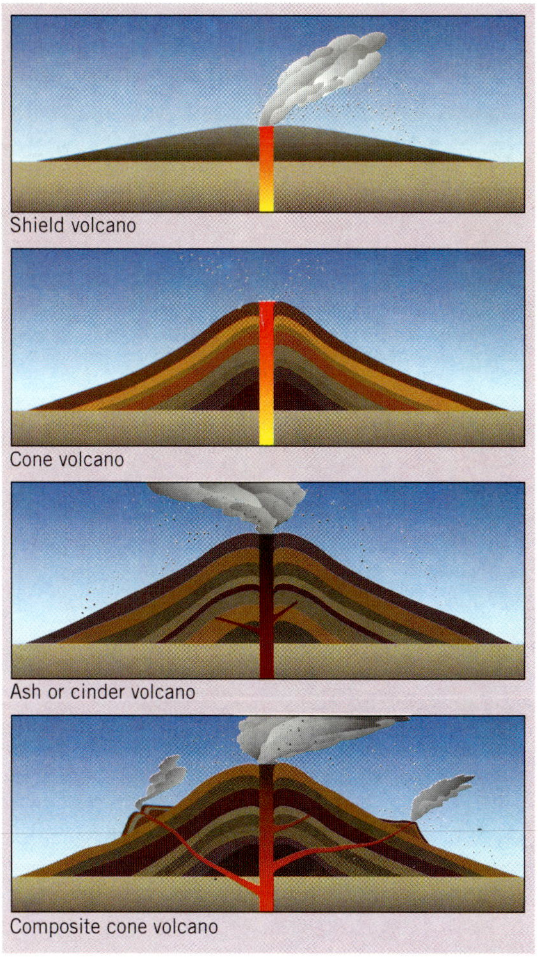

Figure 2

Photograph 1

Activity F

Look at Figure 2 and name the type of volcano below.

Answer like this: 1 *This volcano has steep sides = cone volcano.*

1 This volcano has steep sides =
2 This volcano has low sides =
3 This volcano is made from lava and ash =
4 This volcano is made from ash or cinders =

Activity G

Look at this photograph of a volcano called Anak Krakatau in Indonesia.

1 Write down what kind of volcano you think it is. (Look at Figure 2 to help you.)
2 Write three sentences to explain what is happening in the photograph.

Settlement in Brazil

- Is everyone poor in a developing country?

Buildings can give us a clue.

This section is about land use in Brazil.

Brazil has some very big cities. The cities have parts that are rich and parts that are poor.

Look at these two photographs of São Paulo. They show the rich and poor parts of the same city.

Activity A

Look at Photograph 1. Match the letters on the photograph with the words below.

Road	Bus	Tall building
Cars	Park	

Activity B

Look at Photograph 2. Match the letters on the photograph with the words below.

Road	Homes	City centre
Litter	People	

Activity C

1 Write down three things that you can see in both Photograph 1 and Photograph 2.

2 Write down two things that show Photograph 1 is of a rich part of the city.

3 Write down three things that show Photograph 2 is of a poor part of the city.

Activity D

1 Write down three sentences about what you think it is like living in the area in Photograph 1.

2 Write down three sentences about what you think it is like living in the area in Photograph 2.

Many people in Brazil come from the countryside to the towns and cities to look for work. But there are no houses for them in the cities, so they build their own houses using anything they can find such as wood, cardboard and plastic sheets.

Most of these homes do not have any water, electricity or drains. There are so many of them that large settlements have grown around the cities. In Brazil these settlements are called **favelas**. They are growing around all the big cities in Brazil, and are the homes of the poor. The people who live there are called **squatters**.

In the centre of the cities like São Paulo there are shops and offices (Photograph 3). Most of the jobs are in the centre of the city.

As more and more people leave the countryside, the towns and cities get bigger. This is called **urbanisation**. In Brazil urbanisation is happening faster than it is in many other countries.

There are big differences between parts of the same city in Brazil, and there are also big differences between the cities and the countryside.

Brazil is a land of differences: rich and poor, cities and the countryside, the forest and the desert, the old and the new. It is a land of **contrasts**.

Photograph 3

Activity E

Match the words below with their meanings.

Answer like this: 1 São Paulo is a very big city in Brazil.

Urbanisation	Squatters	Favelas
Contrasts	São Paulo	

1 ____________ is a very big city in Brazil.
2 ____________ is a word that means differences.
3 ____________ are settlements of poor houses.
4 ____________ are people who live in favelas.
5 ____________ means the way towns and cities grow.

Activity F

Copy these sentences and write True or False.

Answer like this: 1 Brazil is a very big country.
True.

1 Brazil is a very big country.
2 Many people move from the countryside to the cities to look for jobs.
3 Favelas are places where rich people live.
4 The cities in Brazil are growing very quickly.
5 Most people in favelas make their own homes.
6 There are big differences between the countryside and the cities in Brazil.
7 There are farms in the centre of São Paulo.

Activity G

Look at Photograph 3 and write down five jobs for people in this part of São Paulo.

Activity H

Use Photographs 1–3 to find three contrasts in Brazil, and write a sentence for each one.

The Rain Forest of Brazil

- What's it like inside a rain forest?

If the trees are cut down the land can change very quickly.

This section is about the rain forest of Brazil.

Like any country, Brazil makes its **wealth** by using the things it has. These things are called its **resources**.

The people are the **human resources**. The climate and land are the **natural resources**. Brazil is very rich in natural resources.

The rain forests are important to Brazil. The rain forest areas of the world are also called **equatorial rain forests**. In Brazil, they may be called the **selvas**.

The rain forests are always hot and wet. This means the climate is **humid**.

The plants and trees grow very quickly in the rain forest. There is no summer or winter at the equator.

It rains every day in the rain forest. The rain is very heavy.

Photograph 1

Activity A

All these sentences about rain forests are true. Copy the sentences which *you can see* are true, by looking at Photograph 1.

Plants and trees grow close together.
It is dark inside the rain forest.
It is hot in the rain forest.
There is very little wind in the rain forest.
It is wet inside the rain forest.
Trees are very tall and straight.
All trees and plants are evergreens.
Trees have very big leaves at the top.
There are creepers hanging from some of the trees.
The rain forest has the same weather every day.
Trees have very few branches in their lower parts.
Fallen leaves rot very quickly.

Activity B

Explain how Photograph 1 shows that each of the sentences you chose from Activity A is true.

Activity C

Copy the sentences that you did not write in your answer to Activity A.

Activity D

Copy and complete these sentences.

1 Humid means ....
2 The selvas in Brazil ....
3 Resources are ....
4 There are no seasons at the equator because ....
5 Inside the rain forest it is ....

Inside the rain forest there is a **balance** between the plants and the soil. The dead leaves fall to the floor of the rain forest. Then the leaves rot in the hot, wet climate. This helps the soil.

If the plants and trees are cut down, the soil may be washed away by the heavy rain. This is called **soil erosion**. If the soil is washed away by the rain, nothing will grow there again. Large areas of the rain forest have been lost in this way (see Photograph 3).

Photograph 2

Photograph 3

Activity E

Look at the trees in Photograph 2. Write three sentences about the shape of the trees.

Activity F

Look at Photograph 3. Write five sentences to explain what you think has happened to this part of the rain forest.

Activity G

Look at Photographs 1, 2 and 3. Copy and complete this chart by writing five good things and five bad things about life inside the rain forest.

What it is like inside the rain forest	
Good things	**Bad things**
1 It is warm all the time.	1 It is dark.

Activity H

1 Use a dictionary to find out what these words mean. Accessible; Musty; Dense; Adapt.
2 Write four sentences about the rain forest to include these words.

Land Use in Italy

- All countries are made up of different areas.

How big are the differences?

This section is about land use in Italy.

Like Brazil, Italy is a land of contrasts. There are big differences between the North of Italy and the South. Look at these photographs.

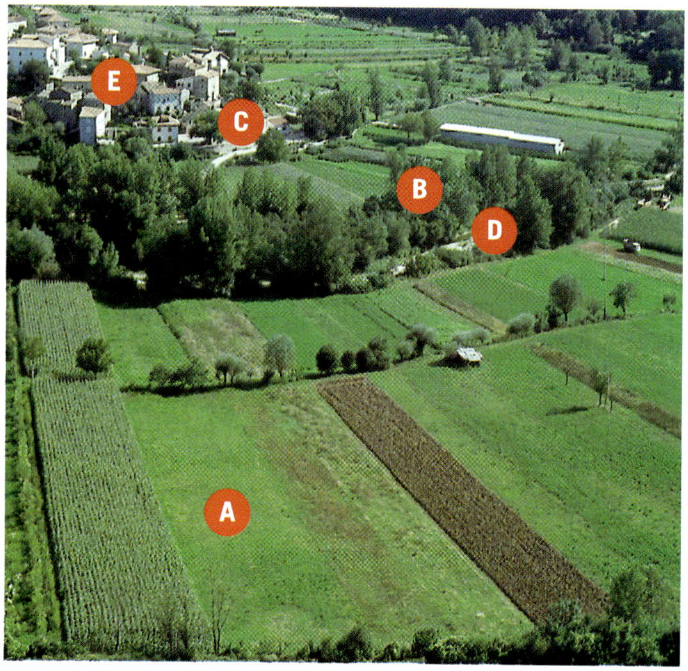

Photograph 1 North Italy

Photograph 2 South Italy

Activity A

Look at Photograph 1 and match the letters on the photograph with the words below.

Answer like this: A = Large, flat fields.

Village	River	Large, flat fields
Trees	Road	

Activity B

Look at Photograph 2 and match the letters on the photograph with the words below.

Steep land	Road	Village
River	Bare slopes	

Activity C

Look at Photographs 1 and 2, and write down if you think you will find the things below in the North or in the South of Italy.

Answer like this:

NORTH OF ITALY	SOUTH OF ITALY
Good soil for growing crops.	Poor soil for growing crops.

Good soil for growing crops.
Poor soil for growing crops.
Land suitable for tractors and machines.
Land not suitable for tractors and machines.
Farms a long way from big towns.
Many big towns not far away.
Old types of farms.
Modern types of farms.

There are also big differences between the towns and cities in the North and South of Italy. Look at Photographs 3 and 4.

Photograph 3 Milan, North Italy

Photograph 4 Naples, South Italy

Activity D

1 Look at Photograph 3 and write down three things that show this is a modern city.

2 Look at Photograph 4 and write down three things that show this is not a modern city.

Activity E

1 Write down two things you can see in both Photograph 3 and Photograph 4.

2 Write down two things you can see only in Photograph 3.

3 Write down two things you can see only in Photograph 4.

Activity F

1 Write down which of the things below you might find in Milan or Naples.

Good roads and good links with other cities.
Poor roads and poor links with other cities.
Few big banks and not much industry.
Many big banks and a great deal of new industry.
Many colleges and good education.
Few colleges and poor education.
An old way of life.
A modern way of life.

2 Write four sentences to explain your answer.

Activity G

Write down three ways you think living in Milan is different to living in Naples.

The Development of Farming

- A country will get rich if it makes the most of what it has.

What happens if it cannot?

This section is about farming in the UK, Brazil and Italy.

A **developed** country or region makes the most of its resources.
A **developing** country or region is improving the use of its resources.

In villages all over the world most people have strong links with farming. In the UK crops are grown and then sold for money. This is called **commercial agriculture**. But in many parts of the world, crops are grown by people for their own food. This is called **subsistence agriculture**.

Look at these photographs of farming in Brazil and Italy.

Photograph 1 Brazil

Photograph 2 Italy

Activity A

Look at Photographs 1 and 2. Copy and complete the chart below.

Things I can see on a farm in Brazil	Things I can see on a farm in Italy

Activity B

Match the worlds below with their meanings.

Developing	Subsistence farming
Commercial farming	Developed

1 __________ means farming for money.
2 __________ means farming for food.
3 __________ means making the most of resources.
4 __________ means improving resources.

A **subsistence** farm does not have many machines. Animals are used instead, and there are many people working on the land. The farms may be small, and a long way from towns and cities. The soil is sometimes not very good and the land may be rocky and steep.

A **commercial** farm has a lot of machines and the land may be flat. The farms may be very big and the soil is usually good.

Photograph 3 Brazil

Photograph 4 Italy

Photograph 5 The UK

Activity C

Look at Photographs 1 and 3 of farms in Brazil.
Copy and complete the chart below.

Things that are the same in Photographs 1 and 3	Things that are different in Photographs 1 and 3

Activity D

Look at Photographs 2 and 4 of farms in Italy.
Copy and complete the chart below.

Things that are the same in Photographs 2 and 4	Things that are different in Photographs 2 and 4

Activity E

1 Look at Photographs 1 to 5. Write down if the farms are subsistence farms or commercial farms.

Answer like this: Photograph 1 is a commercial farm.

2 Give reasons for each of your answers.

Answer like this: There is a tractor in Photograph 1.

The Selvas 1

- Sometimes it is easier to draw something than write about it.

This is how to do it.

This section is about the rain forest in Brazil.

Look at this photograph of the selvas or rain forest. This area has not been developed in any way.

Photograph 1

To draw a sketch of the photograph, follow these steps.

Step 1: Draw a box the same size as the photograph. (Look at Figure 1.)

Step 2: Mark the box into four parts, like the lines A to B and C to D.

Step 3: Draw in the important outlines. This sketch has been started for you.

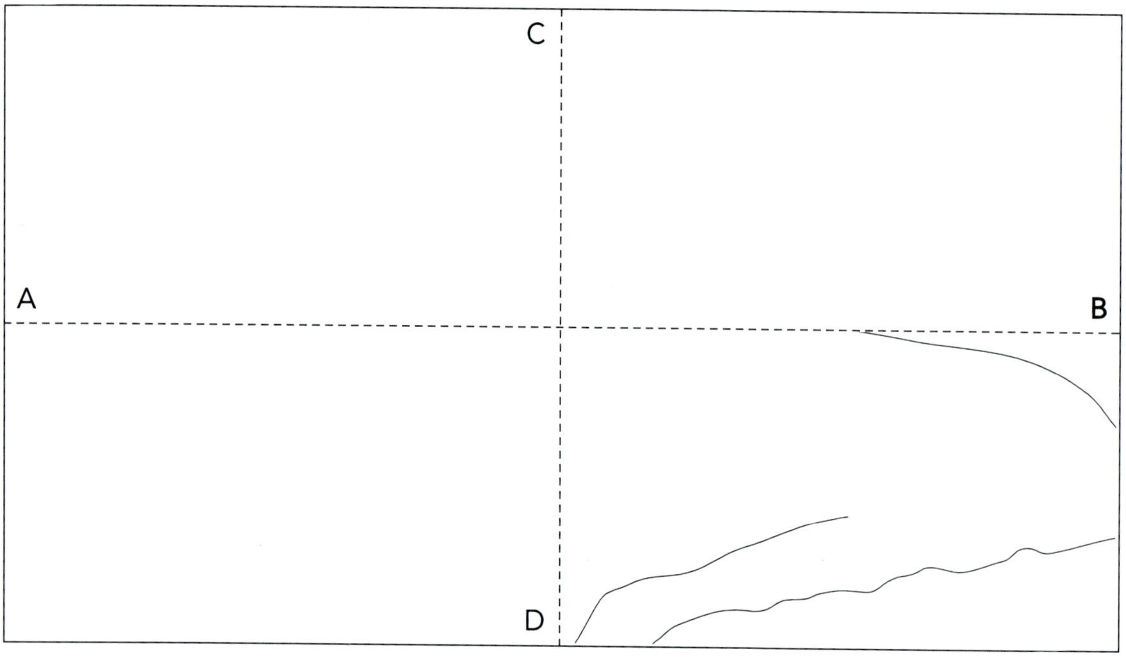

Figure 1

The climate of the rain forest is hot and wet all year round. It is a good climate for plants to grow thick and fast.

This means that plants **compete** with each other for sunlight and rain. The tallest trees in the rain forest are special:

1 They are very tall and grow straight up towards the sun.

2 At the bottom of the trees there are **buttress** roots to keep them straight so that they do not fall over.

3 The leaves at the top are very wide so that they get plenty of sun.

4 The leaves grow right across the top of the trees, to make a **canopy** (Figure 2). This cuts out the sunlight lower down.

5 The trees do not have many branches or leaves lower down because the canopy cuts out the sun.

6 The leaves get rid of the heavy rain by growing a drip tip (Figure 2 shows a drip tip leaf and an ordinary leaf).

7 Creeper plants called **lianas** grow around the tall trees.

Figure 2 A rain forest tree

Figure 3

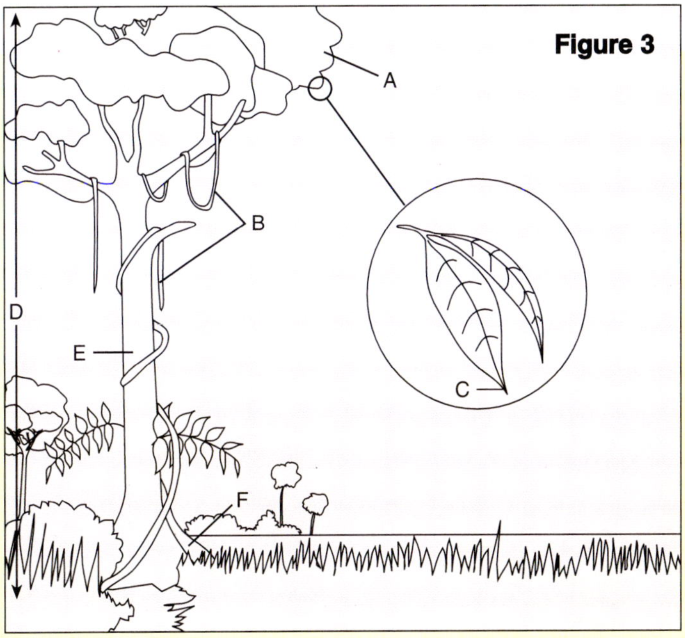

Activity A

Copy and complete Figure 1.

Activity B

1 Match the letters on Figure 3 with the words below.

Canopy	Liana	Buttress roots
No branches	Very tall	Drip tips

2 Draw and label the sketch in Figure 3.

Activity C

Copy the sketch of a drip tip and explain how it works.

The Selvas 2

- The rain forest looks very thick, but is it all the same inside?

  Let's take a look.

This section is more about the rain forest in Brazil.

Look at this photograph of the rain forest.

There are three layers of vegetation in the rain forest.

The sketch of the rain forest (Figure 1) shows the three layers. The top layer is made up of the very tall trees. The canopy cuts out the light lower down.

In the middle layer the trees are not as big because there is not as much light. The trees grow very quickly where the light does break through.

Photograph 1

Figure 1

The forest floor is covered with dead leaves and dead plants. There is not much light inside the forest so there is very little **undergrowth** or small plants. In places where there is some light, the undergrowth is thick. This happens where there is a clearing in the forest and near rivers.

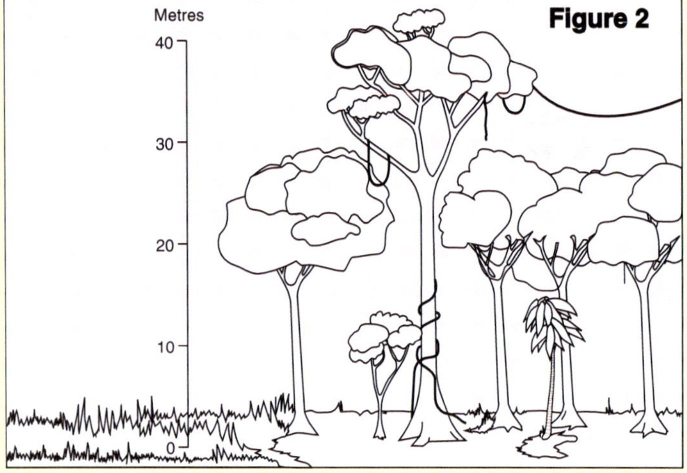

Figure 2

Activity A

Copy and complete the sketch in Figure 2.

Activity B

Match the words in the box with the words below.

The top layer	The middle layer	The bottom layer

1 ______________________ has forest litter, little undergrowth and is below ten metres in height.

2 ______________________ is above 30 metres tall, and made up of the giant trees with a large canopy.

3 ______________________ is between 10 and 30 metres in height and made up of small trees where sunlight breaks through.

Photograph 2 A Kayapo Indian village in the rain forest, next to the River Xingu

Indian villages in the rain forest are often near the rivers. The rivers are important for fishing and for transport. There are also some villages in the thick of the forest.

The forest is cleared and the groups of families farm the land. The men hunt in the forest. After a while the people move to another part of the forest and start again.

But this way of life is changing for the Indians. The outside world, with new farming and industry, is bringing a new way of life. Not all the Indian groups are happy with these changes.

Activity C

Draw a sketch of the Kayapo Indian village shown in Photograph 2. Label the following on your sketch.

River	Thick forest	Village huts
Forest track	Village clearing	

Activity D

Write down three differences between the village in Photograph 2 and a village in this country.

Activity E

Why do you think some of the Indian groups do not want to change their way of life? Give three reasons.

Land Use in the UK

- Where are the most beautiful parts of the UK?

  Let's take a look at the National Parks.

This section is about the countryside in the UK.

There are many beautiful parts of the UK. Some of the most beautiful parts are called National Parks.

Photograph 1

Look at this photograph of a National Park. Try to find these things in the photograph: the lake, the mountains, the forest, the grassland, the farm track and the gate.

Activity A

Copy Figure 1 and colour your drawing.

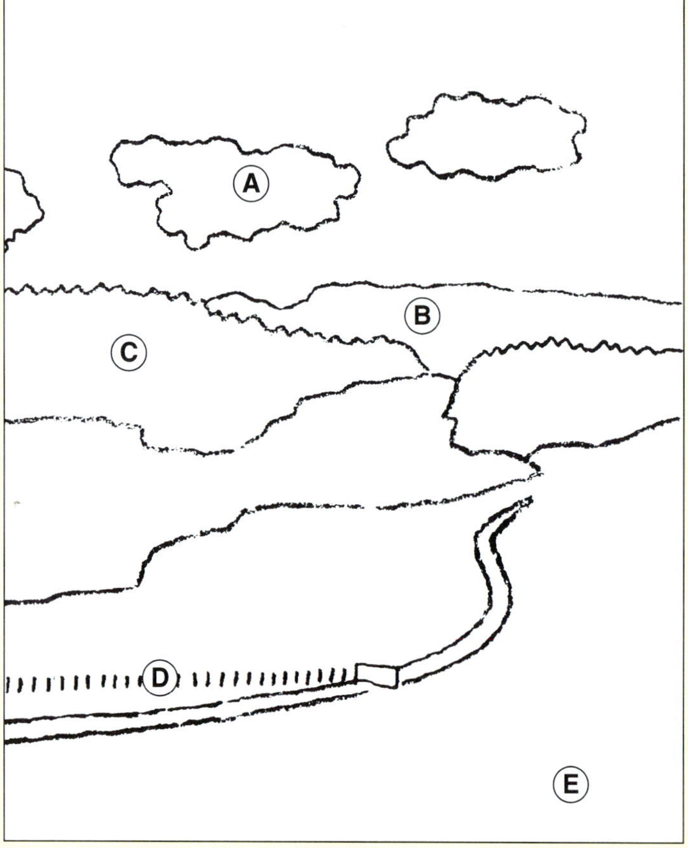

Figure 1

Activity B

Match the letters on Figure 1 with the words below.

Answer like this: A = Clouds.

Grassland	Fence	Forest
Mountains	Clouds	

Activity C

1 Write the letters F, G and H on your sketch to show three more things.

2 Write down what the letters show.

National Parks are places where people can enjoy the beautiful landscape. There is not much industry in a National Park, so the landscape can be natural for people and the animals.

Most National Parks are in highland areas where there are no big cities. In a National Park the landscape can be looked after for everyone to enjoy. National Parks are places of peace and quiet.

A lot of people like to go to visit a National Park just for the day. Other people may stay for a longer holiday. If too many tourists visit a National Park there are problems. The roads get too busy, and not all the tourists look after the countryside. This can make things difficult for farmers and for the animals.

A National Park has to be developed carefully. Look at Figure 3. It shows the area in Photograph 1 after it has been developed.

Figure 2 National Parks in England and Wales

Activity D

Look at Figure 2 and answer the following questions.

1 Name two National Parks in South-West England.
2 Name a National Park in North-West England.
3 Name a National Park in North-East England.
4 Name three National Parks in Wales.
5 Name the National Park nearest your home.

Activity E

1 Copy Figure 3.
2 Label your sketch with the words below.

Caravan park	Car park	Boats	Café
Factory	Road	Farmland	

3 Do you think this National Park has been developed properly? Write three sentences to explain your answer.
4 Write about how you would spend a day trip at a National Park.

Figure 3

Development in Italy

- Can a sketch help us to sum up a place?

This is how to do it.

This section is about the more developed and less developed parts of Italy.

The most developed part of Italy is the North. Look at this photograph of the North Italian Plain. It shows the way the land has been developed near the River Po.

Figure 1 is called a **land use sketch**. It shows the way the land has been used in this part of Italy.

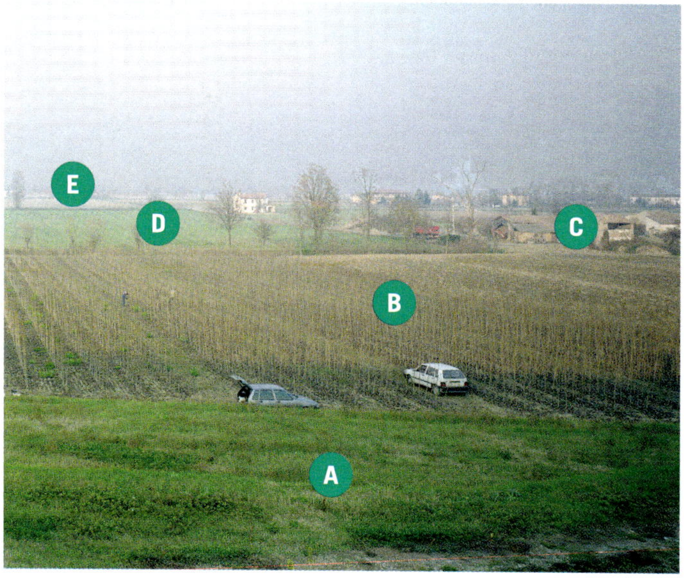

Photograph 1

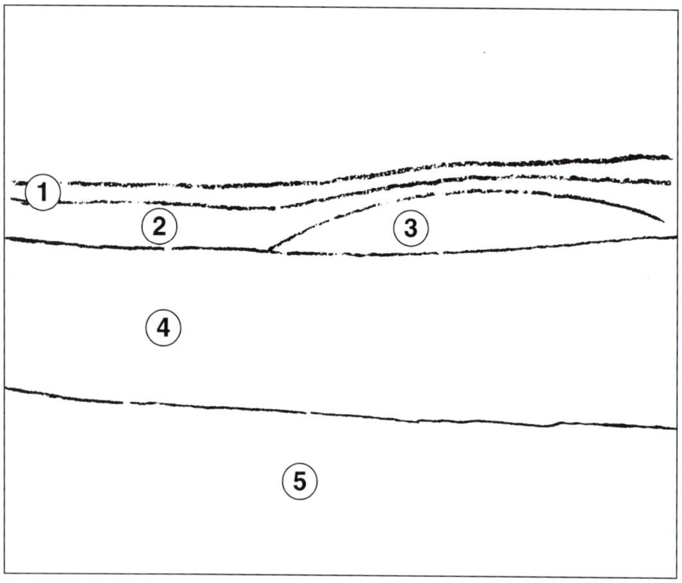

Figure 1

Activity A

Look at Photograph 1. Match the letters A – E with the words below.

Tall vines growing in rows
Settlement on higher ground
Rich green rough pasture
Flat fields of crops
Town in far distance

Activity B

Write five sentences about what you can see in Photograph 1.

Activity C

Look at the land use sketch. Match the numbers on the sketch with the words below.

Settlement on higher ground
Tall vines growing in rows
Town in far distance
Flat fields of crops
Rich green rough pasture

Activity D

1 Copy the land use sketch (Figure 1).
2 Colour your land use sketch.
3 Use a key to show what the colours mean, like this:

■ Rich green rough pasture

The less developed part of Italy is the Mezzogiorno in the South. There is less industry than in the North, and there is also less commercial farming.

However, the Mezzogiorno is also a beautiful part of Italy. The hot, dry Mediterranean summer weather means that it is a good area to go to for a holiday. So the tourist industry has helped to bring jobs to the South. But the Mezzogiorno is a poor area so tourism is still under-developed.

Some parts of the South, like the Bay of Naples and the island of Capri, have always had many tourists.

Look at Photograph 2. It shows part of the Bay of Naples.

Photograph 2

Activity E

1 Copy and complete the land use sketch of the Bay of Naples (Figure 2).
2 Label your sketch using the words below.

Bay of Naples	Clear blue sky	
Hotels	Jetty	Marina

Activity F

Look at Photograph 2. Name ten jobs that people in this area could do for tourists.

Activity G

Draw a holiday poster for the South of Italy showing that it is a good place to go for a holiday.

Activity H

How would you develop tourism in the South of Italy? Write down five things you would do to encourage more people to visit the region.

Figure 2

Farming in the UK

- How easy is it to draw a map?

Let's start by copying one.

This section is about farming in parts of the UK.

Crops like potatoes and wheat are grown as food for people. Other crops may be grown to feed animals. These are called **fodder crops**.

Photograph 1 shows an **arable farm**. An arable farmer grows food crops like vegetables and cereals. Wheat, barley and oats are cereal crops. East Anglia is a good place for arable farming.

Photograph 1

Photograph 2 shows a **dairy farm**. Dairy cows give milk. Milk is an important food and is also used to make butter, cheese, cream and yoghurt.

Photograph 2

Some places have dairy farms and grow crops as well. This is called **mixed farming**.

A **market garden** grows vegetables, flowers and fruit. Sometimes greenhouses are used on a market garden. Growing plants and vegetables under glass keeps them warm.

Photograph 3 shows a **hill farm**. A hill farmer looks after sheep and some beef cattle. Sheep farms are located in the hills and mountains of the UK. The weather is too cold and wet to grow many crops. The land is too steep and the soil is too thin and stony for crops.

Photograph 3

Activity A

Copy and complete the sentences below.

Answer like this: 1 Arable farming means growing crops.

1 (Arable / dairy) farming means growing crops.
2 A fodder crop is for (people / animals).
3 (Milk / vegetables) comes from a dairy farm.
4 A market garden grows (vegetables / cheese).
5 Sheep are found on a (hill / market) farm.
6 A hill farm has (good / poor) soil.
7 Dairy farms have lots of (cows / sheep).
8 Arable farms use (tractors / cars) in their fields.

Activity B

1 Name three things made from milk.
2 Name three things grown on a market garden.
3 Name three cereal crops.

Activity C

Look at the photographs.

1 Write three sentences about an arable farm.
2 Write three sentences about a dairy farm.
3 Write three sentences about a hill farm.

A map of the UK's farming areas can be copied using a grid.

Look at this map of England, Scotland and Wales (Figure 1). It can be copied using the grid as a guideline, like this:

Figure 1

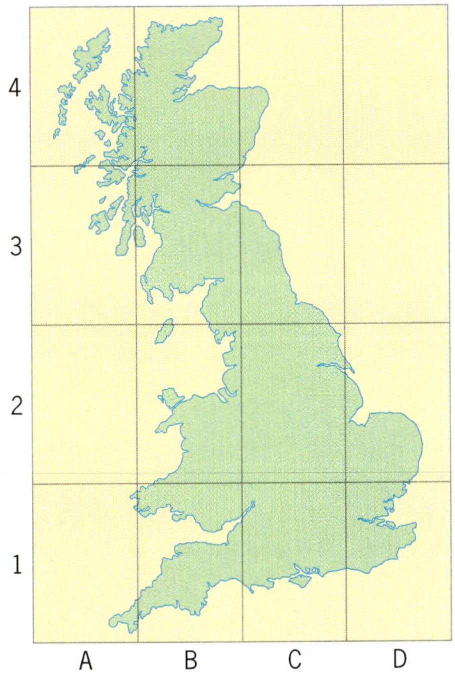

Step 1: Draw a grid the same size as Figure 1. (See Figure 2.)

Figure 2

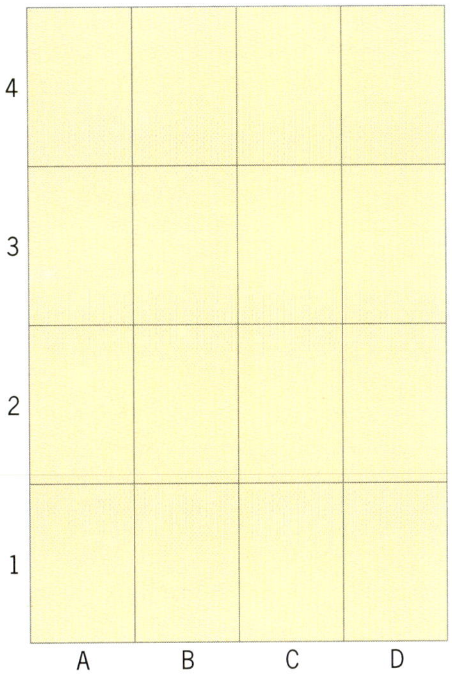

Step 2: Copy the map outline on your grid, one square at a time. In Figure 3, the squares D1 and C3 have been completed for you.

Figure 3

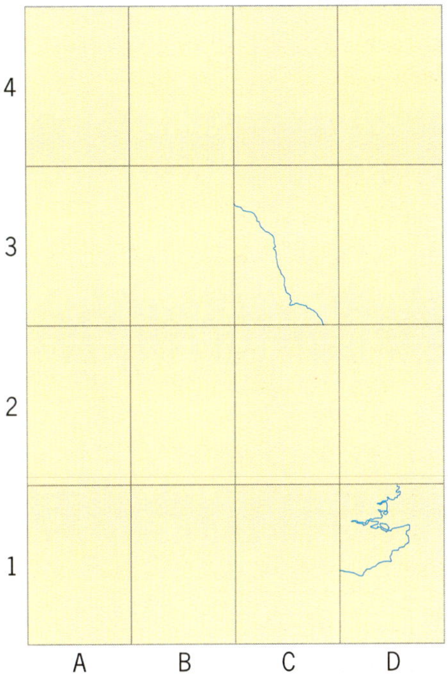

Activity D

1. Draw a grid the same size as Figure 1.
2. Use your grid to copy Figure 3.
3. Use your grid to complete the map of England, Scotland and Wales.

Activity E

Use your map from Activity D and copy the farming areas of England, Scotland and Wales (Figure 4).

Activity F

Write ten sentences about farming in the UK, using your map to help you.

Figure 4

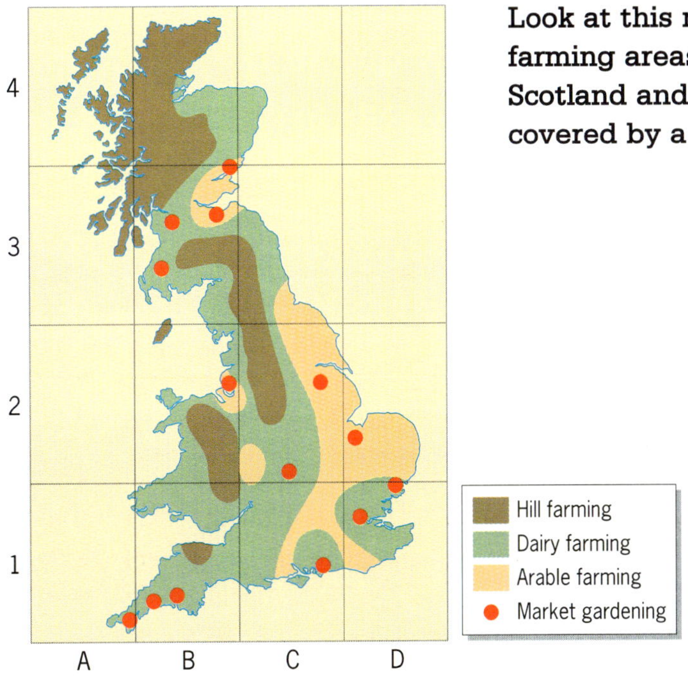

Look at this map showing the farming areas in England, Scotland and Wales. It is covered by a grid.

Farming in Brazil

- Maps do not always have to be perfect.

  A sketch map is a quick way of drawing one.

This section is about farming in Brazil.

Much of the farming in Brazil is subsistence farming, where the animals and crops are for family food.

In some parts of the rain forest small areas are cleared by the people who live in the forest (Photograph 1). They hunt in the forest and grow crops until the soil is no longer any good. Then the families will move on to another part of the forest and start again. This type of subsistence farming is called **shifting cultivation**.

Photograph 1

There are also parts of Brazil where there is commercial farming. Some of this is on very large farms called **plantations** or **fazendas**. On these very large farms most of the money comes from growing one crop, like coffee (Photograph 2) or sugar. Brazil grows more coffee beans than any other country in the world. But it is a big risk to depend on just one crop, so now farmers may grow other things as well.

Photograph 2

Brazil is a very big country and there are many other kinds of farming. Large areas of the rain forest have been cleared to make way for cattle and grasslands, and there are many kinds of crops in other areas.

Activity A

Copy and complete the sentences below.

Answer like this: 1 *Growing crops for food is called subsistence farming.*

1 Growing crops for food is called (commercial / subsistence) farming.
2 Moving from one part of the forest to another is called shifting (growing / cultivation).
3 A plantation is a (small / large) farm.
4 Brazil grows more (coffee / baked) beans than any other country in the world.
5 It is (safe / risky) to grow only one crop.

Activity B

1 Write three sentences about the shifting cultivation in Photograph 1.
2 Write three sentences about the plantation farming in Photograph 2.

Activity C

1 Use a dictionary and write down the meanings of these words: cultivation; shifting.
2 Why do you think the farming in Photograph 1 is called shifting cultivation?

Drawing a map can take a long time, so we sometimes draw a **sketch map**. A sketch map is a quick and simple way of drawing a map. It does not show the exact shape of the country. Look at these maps of Brazil. Figures 2, 3 and 4 are sketch maps.

A sketch map shows only the main points on the outline of the map. Figure 3 shows the main kinds of farming in Brazil.

Figure 1

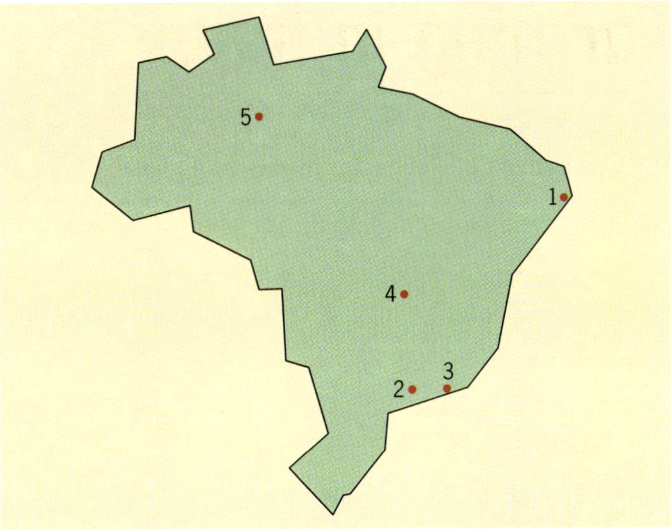

Figure 2

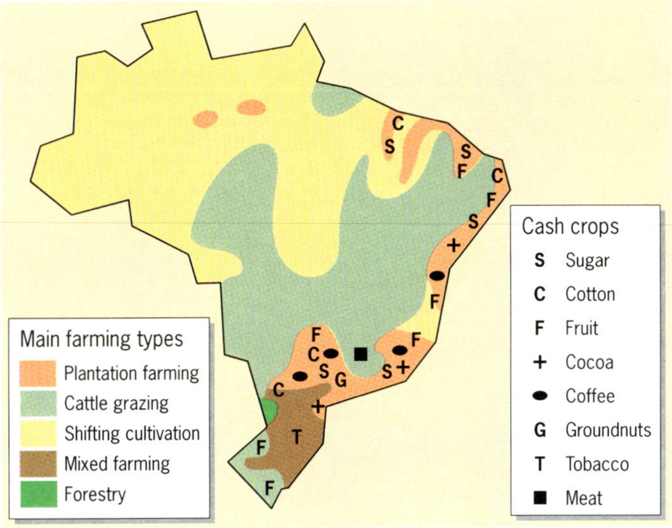

Figure 3

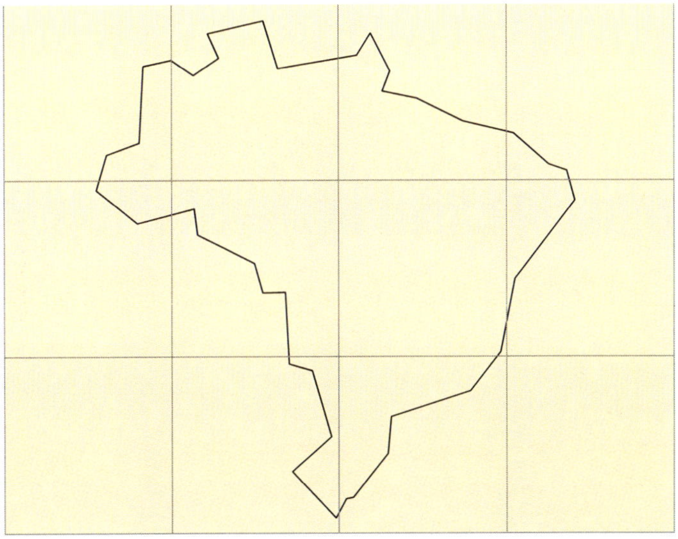

Figure 4

Activity D

Name the cities in Figure 2.

Answer like this: 1 = Recife

Activity E

1 Draw a grid the same size as Figure 4.

2 Use your grid to copy Figure 4.

Activity F

On your sketch map of Brazil, colour the following farming areas.

1 Shifting cultivation
2 Plantation farming
3 Cattle grazing
4 Coffee

Activity G

Write a sentence about the location of the farming areas you have marked on your sketch map.

Farming in Italy

- Maps and photographs can work together to show the geography of a country.

Let's look at Italy.

This section is about farming in Italy.

Look at these photographs of farming in Italy:

Photograph 1

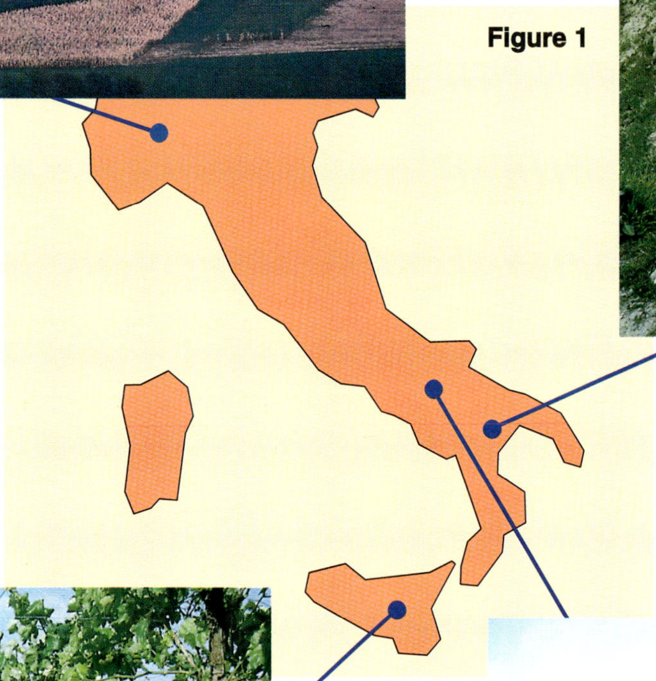

Figure 1

Photograph 2

Photograph 3

Photograph 4

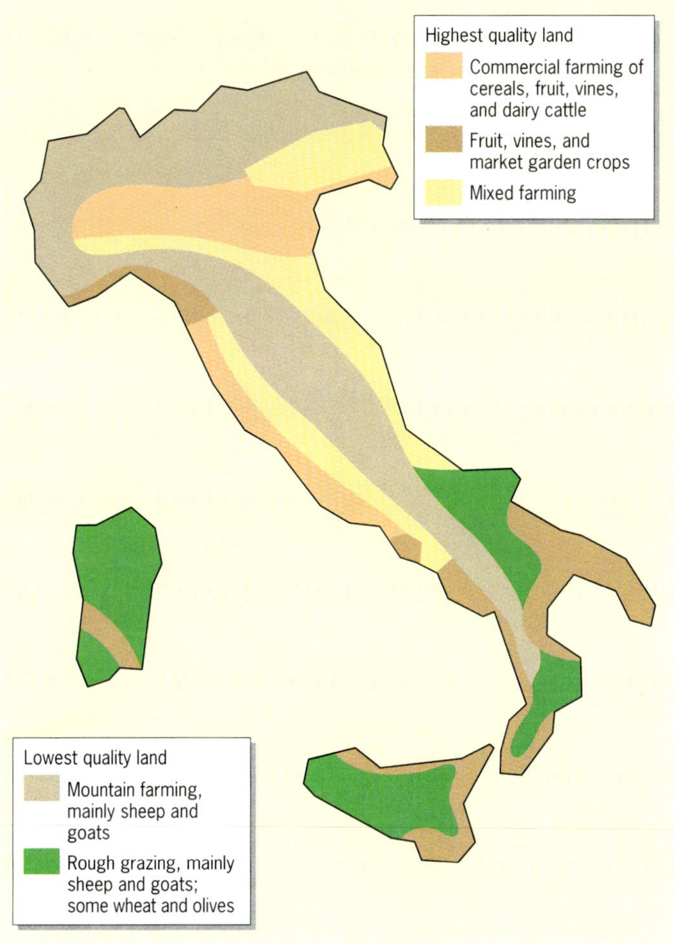

Figure 2 Farming in Italy

Figure 3 Europe

Activity A

Look at page 42. Copy the sketch map of Italy, and draw sketches of the photographs. Make them the same size as they are on page 42, and set them out in the same way.

Activity B

Look at Figure 2, and match the photographs on page 42 with the writing below.

Photograph 1	Photograph 2
Photograph 3	Photograph 4

- ____________ shows rough grazing in the South of Italy. The land is very hilly, and farming is mainly sheep and goats, with some wheat and olive growing. The poor soils mean that farming in the area is not very good. Most of the farms are small.
- ____________ shows commercial arable farming in Italy's most important crop-growing area – the North Italian Plain. The flat land is good for machines, and the rich soil and irrigation mean that there are big, modern farms.
- ____________ shows the highest slopes of the Apennine Mountains, which run down the centre of Italy. The bare slopes on the mountain sides show where the soil has been washed away. Trees have been cut from these mountains for many years.
- ____________ shows vineyards on the island of Sicily. Flat land is made by cutting terraces in the hillsides, like very large steps. This is an important wine-making area. The grapes grow well in the hot, dry Mediterranean climate.

Activity C

1 Copy Figure 2.
2 On your sketch map of Italy, mark these cities.

Milan	Turin	Genoa	Rome
Naples	Venice	Cagliari	Palermo

Activity D

1 Copy the simple sketch map of Europe (Figure 3), Without the boundaries.
2 Name Italy and the UK on your sketch map.

The Scale of the British Isles

- What is the link between two things that have the same shape, but are a different size?

The answer is scale.

This section is about understanding how maps show the size of a country.

Look at the photograph and the map below. They show the same area. Everything on the photograph and the map has been reduced, or made smaller 1500 times. But everything on the map is the same shape as it is in the photograph.

The link between the size of an object and its shape is called **scale**. The scale of this map is 1 : 1500.

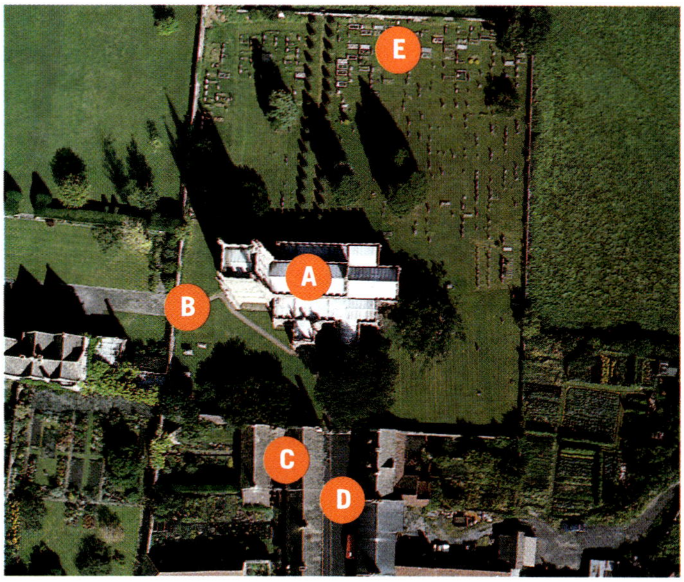

Photograph 1

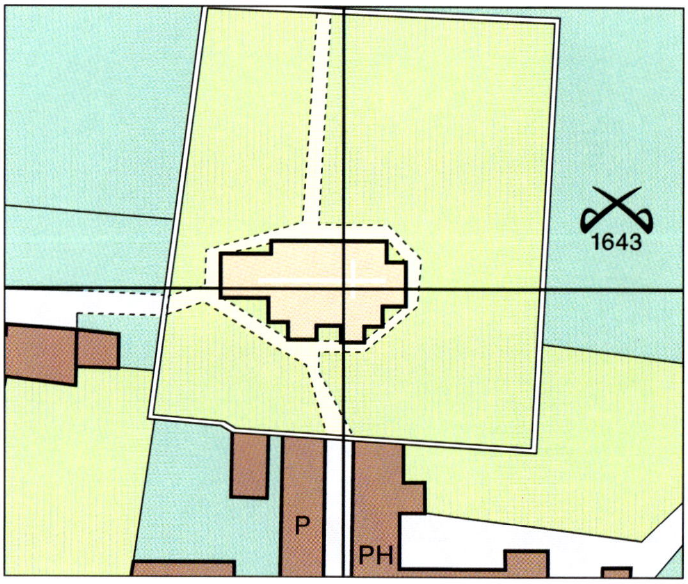

Figure 1

Activity A

Look at Photograph 1 and match the letters with the words below.

Houses	Church	Path
Road	Churchyard	

Activity B

1. Write down two things you can see in the photograph that are not on the map.
2. Write down two things you can see on the map that are not in the photograph.

Activity C

Look at the reduced map (Figure 2). Use the grids as a guide to copy and complete the map.

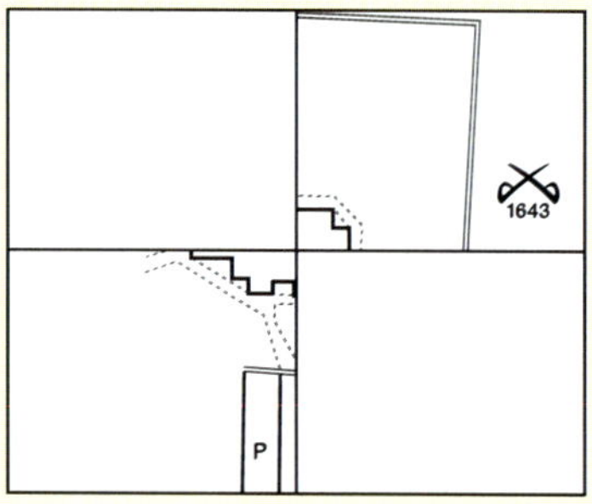

Figure 2

Activity D

Copy and complete these sentences.

1. Figure 2 is (half / twice) the size of Figure 1.
2. The scale of Figure 2 is (1 : 750 / 1 : 3000).

The scale of a map can be changed by using grids. Look at this map of the British Isles. The scale is 1 : 10 000 000.

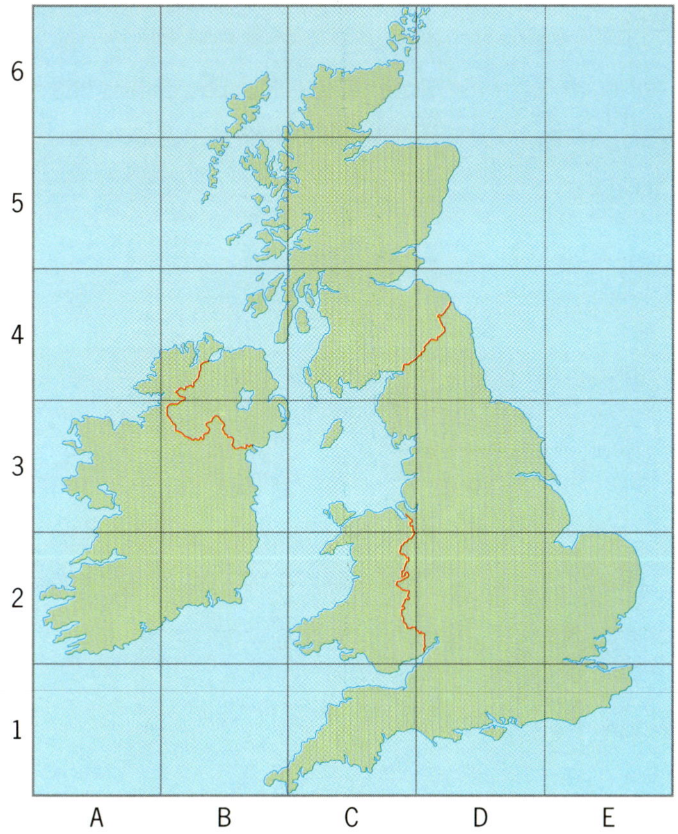

Figure 3

Figure 4 shows the same grid pattern, but the grids are a different size. These grids are half the size, so the scale of the map in Figure 4 is 1 : 20 000 000.

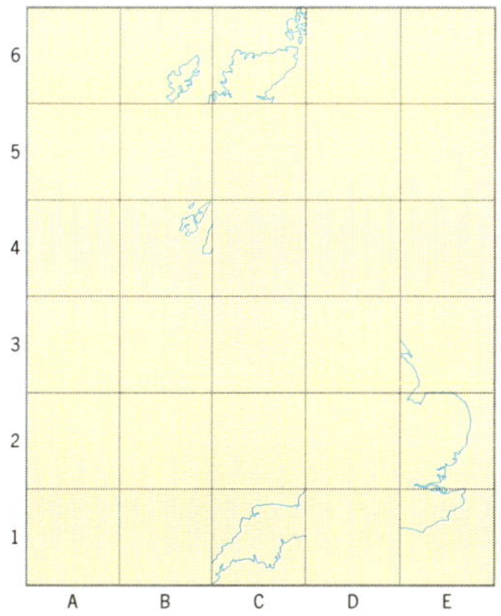

Figure 4

Activity E

Look at these maps. Name the maps with the same scales.

1

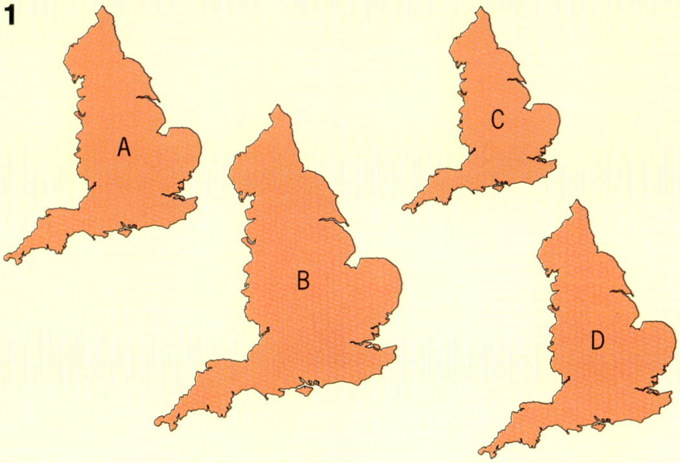

2

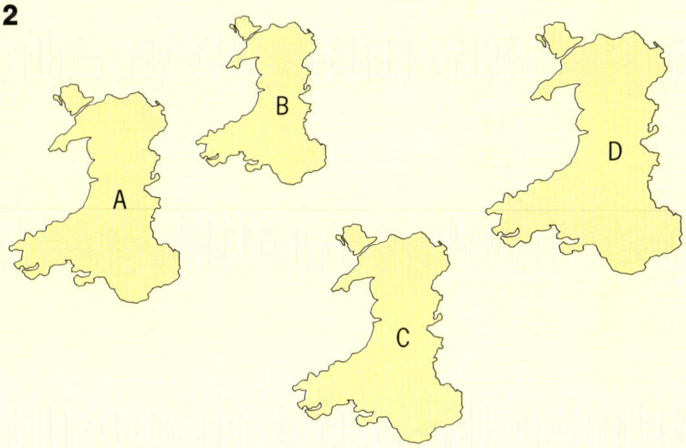

3

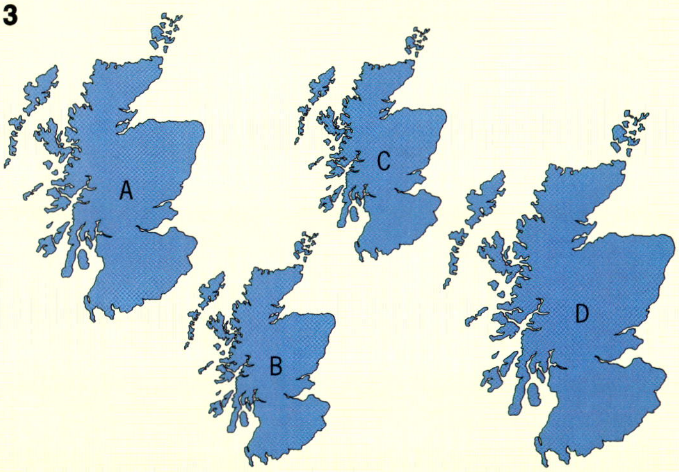

Activity F

1 Copy the grid pattern in Figure 4.

2 Use the grid pattern to draw a map of the British Isles to a scale of 1 : 20 000 000.

The Scale of Brazil

- To understand Brazil, we need to understand its size.

Let's take a look at the scale of Brazil.

This section uses scale to look at the geography of Brazil.

Brazil is a big country. It is the fifth largest country in the world, and more than 30 times larger than the UK. Brazil is so big that it is next to ten other countries, and takes up nearly half of South America.

Brazil is very rich in natural resources. These include iron ore, coal and other minerals, oil, gas, timber and plenty of water.

There are five regions in Brazil. Look at Figure 1.

Figure 1

This is the North region taken from Figure 1.

This is a map of the British Isles drawn to the same scale.

Activity A

Look at the map of Brazil (Figure 1). What is the scale of the map?

Activity B

1 Name the largest region in Brazil.
2 Name the smallest region in Brazil.
3 Name any region smaller than the British Isles.
4 Name the regions larger than the British Isles.

Activity C

Copy and complete the sentences below.

1 Brazil is a very (small / big) country.
2 Brazil is more than (30 / 60) times larger than the UK.
3 (All / Some) of the regions in Brazil are larger than the UK.
4 Most of the rain forest of Brazil is in the (North / South) region.

Activity D

Match the maps with the same scale.

Answer like this: **1** The matching scales are ________ and ________ .

1

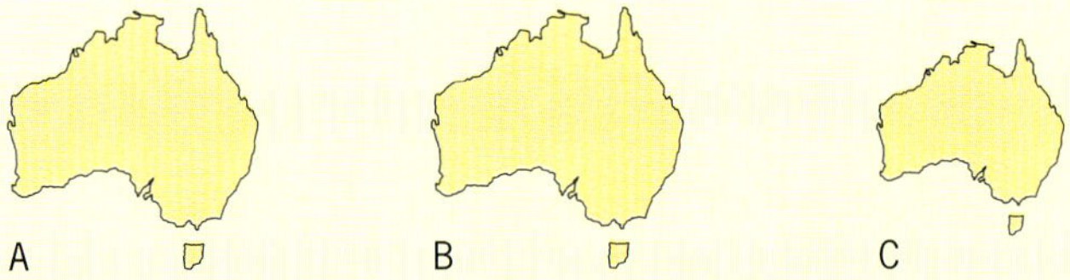

2

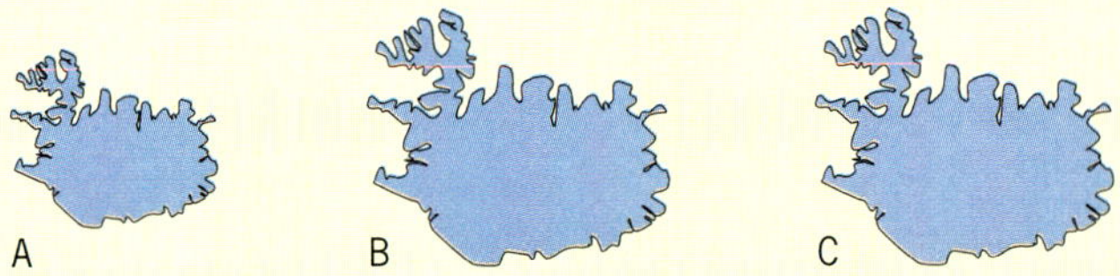

3

Photograph 1 Tucuri Dam

Brazil has many big rivers, like the River Amazon and the River Parana. Power from the water in the rivers can be used to make electricity.

This is called **hydro-electric power, or HEP** for short. The electricity is used for industry and to help develop Brazil.

But, there are problems when the development is not planned properly.

The **waste** from industry may be fed back into the rivers. This means the water is not fit to drink and fish are killed. The people of the forests need the river for their way of life.

Land used for mining may also be destroyed. In some areas it may be destroyed forever.

People may have to leave their homes when a dam is built across the river to make HEP, as the land is flooded. They do not always want to move. The homes of the animals are also flooded when a dam is built.

The towns that come with the new developments do not always bring a better life for the people who live there. A lot of the money goes to big companies.

Brazil is such a big country and has so many natural resources that it can become very rich, but only if the development is planned.

Figure 2 Brazil's rivers

Activity E

Look at Figure 2.

1 What is the scale of this map of Brazil?
2 Name five rivers in Brazil.
3 Name three rivers in Brazil which are longer than the UK.

Activity F

Look at Photograph 1 and write down five sentences to describe what is happening to the river.

Activity G

Write down what you think these two people would go on to say about new development in the rain forest.

Western Europe and the EU

- Small countries sometimes work together to overcome their size.

Let's look at the scale of Europe.

This section is about Western Europe.

The countries of Europe are smaller than Brazil. Look at these two maps of Western Europe and Brazil. They are the same scale.

The countries of Western Europe are more developed than Brazil. There is more industry in Europe than there is in Brazil.

With so much industry in Europe, much waste goes into the rivers. This means that there is a great deal of pollution in the rivers, just like parts of Brazil.

Figure 1 Western Europe

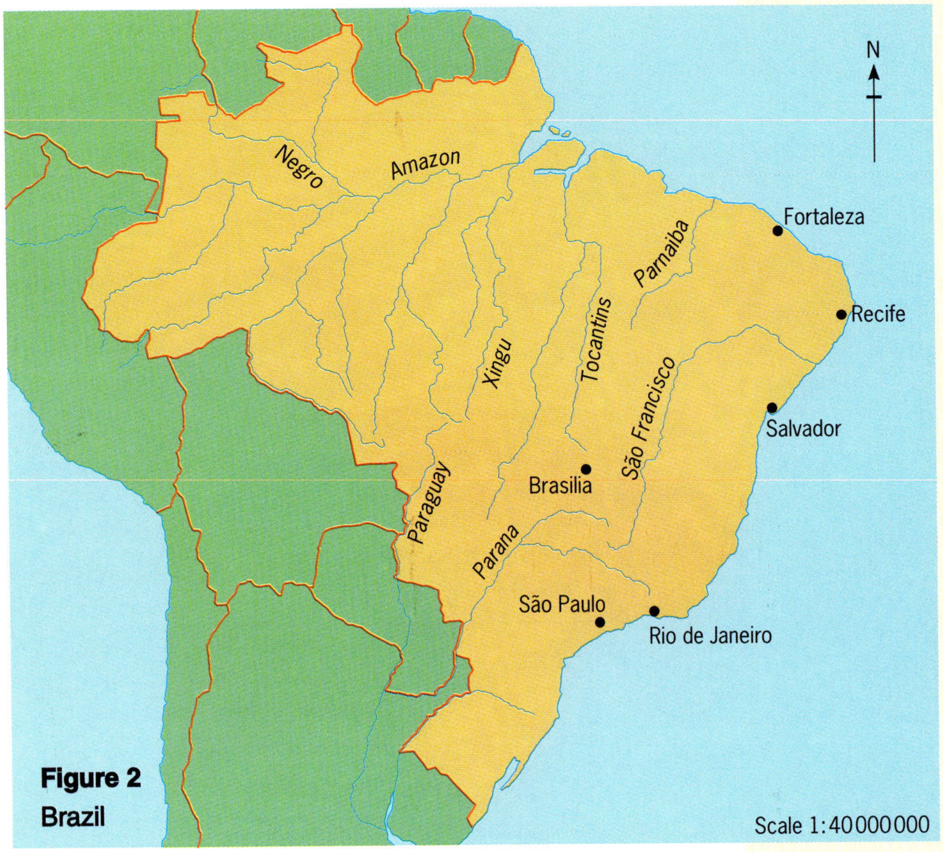

Figure 2
Brazil

Activity A

1 Look at Figure 1 and Figure 2. What is the scale of the two maps?
2 Which is bigger, Brazil or the UK?
3 Name the smallest country in Figure 1.
4 Name the largest country in Figure 1.

Activity B

Which of the countries below are drawn at the same scale as they are in Figure 1?

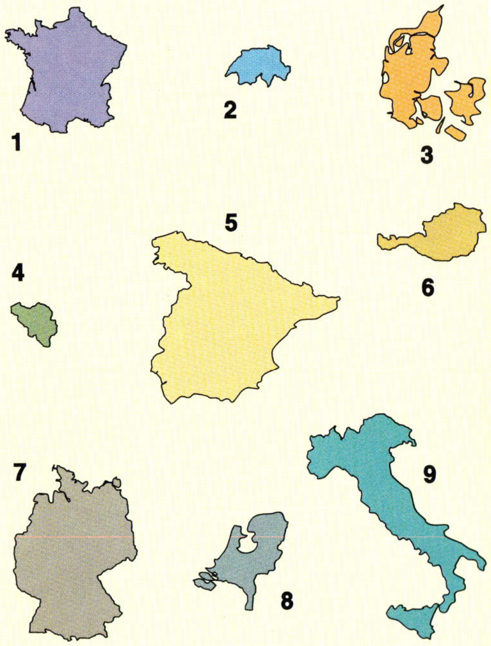

Activity C

How many times bigger than the UK is Brazil? Is it 10 times, 35 times, or 100 times?

Some countries in Western Europe buy and sell things to each other in a special way. This group of countries is called the **European Union,** or **EU** for short.

They work together, as if they are one big country. This is because the countries of Western Europe are not as big as countries like the USA, Russia, China or Brazil.

There are fifteen countries in the EU. These countries are shown in Figure 3.

The EU is not just about work and jobs. It is also about the care of the environment. This means looking after rivers. The EU helps to make sure that rivers are not polluted by industry.

The EU gives money to help develop parts of Europe. The Mezzogiorno is one of these areas.

The countries of the EU work together in many other ways too. They help to look after farming, tourism and other parts of the world.

There may even be a time when the countries in the EU try to join together to make one big country. Many people would not like this. How about you?

Figure 3
The European Union

Photograph 1

Activity D

Look at Figure 3. Make a list of the EU countries and their capital cities.

Answer like this: COUNTRY — CAPITAL CITY
France — Paris

Activity E

List the five ways that EU countries work together.

Activity F

1 Name the biggest country in the EU.
2 Is the UK an EU country?
3 Which is larger, Brazil or all the countries in the EU put together?

Activity G

1 Write three sentences about the pollution in Photograph 1.
2 What would you do to an industry that does not take care of the environment? Write down three things.

Activity H

Do you think the countries of the EU should join together to make one country? Write down five sentences to explain your answer.

Distance and Cities

- Measuring long distances on a map is not always easy.

This is how to make it easy.

This section is about measuring distances on small scale maps.

Measuring distances on a map with a small scale can be difficult. Look at this map of the world.

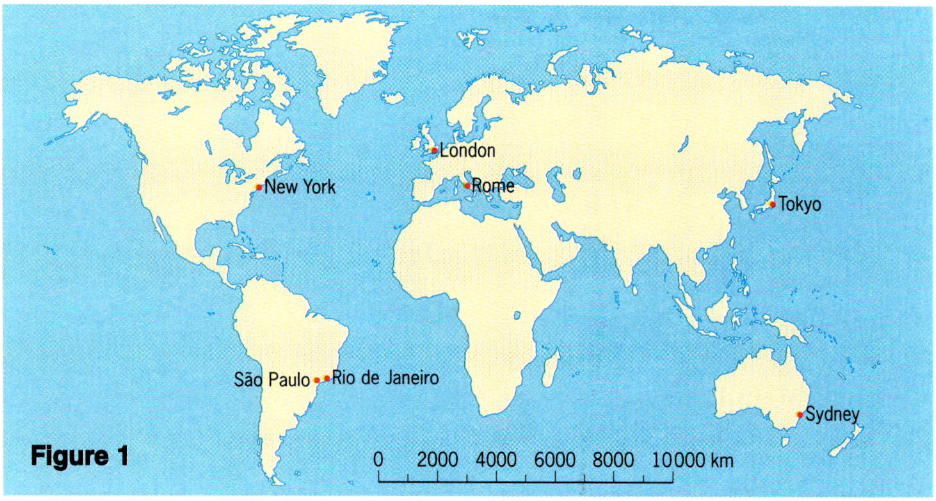

Figure 1

The distance between London and Rio de Janeiro can be measured like this:

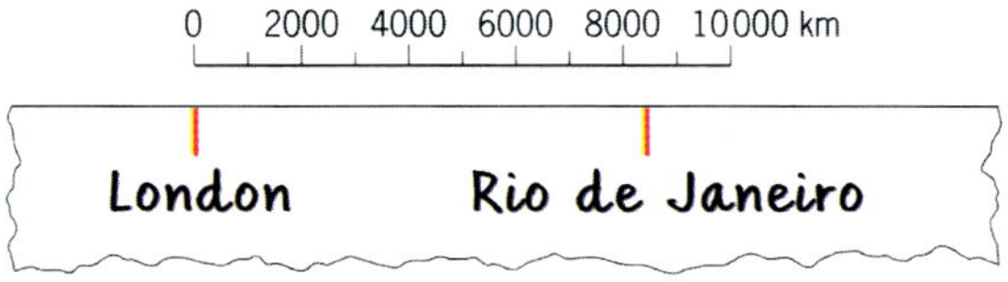

The distance between London and Rio de Janeiro can be rounded off to 8000 kilometres. This means that the distance is measured to the nearest thousand kilometres, on the scale line.

Activity A

Look at these distances and round them off to the nearest **hundred** kilometres.

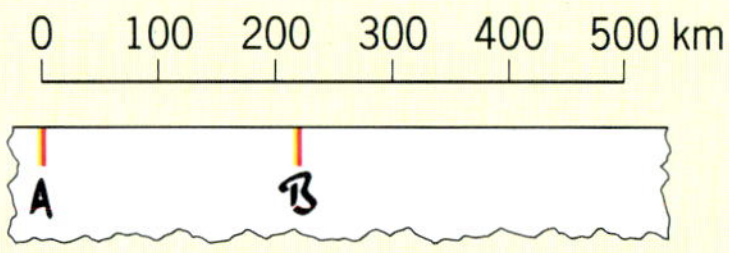

1

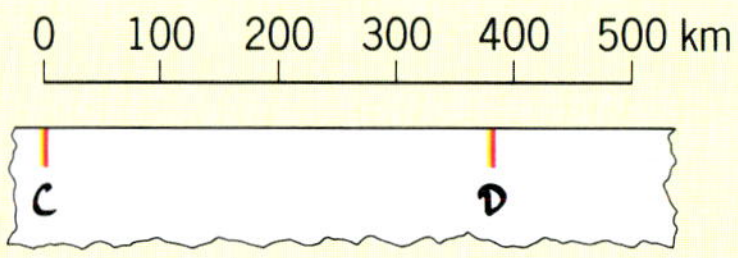

2

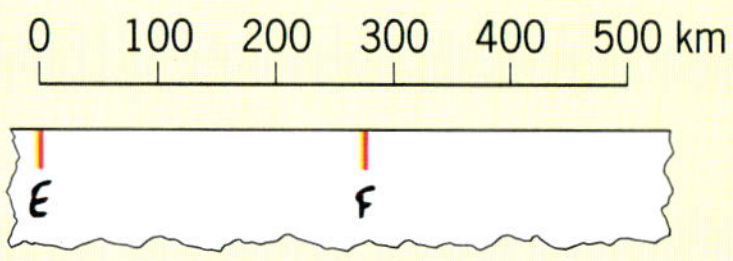

3

Activity B

Look at these distances and round them off to the nearest **thousand** kilometres.

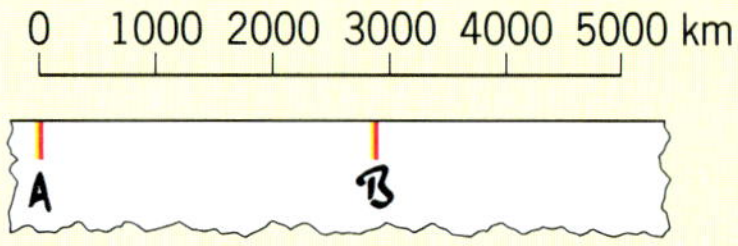

1

2

3

Activity C

Round off these distances to the nearest hundred kilometres.

Answer like this: 1 = *600*km

1 580km
2 430km
3 790km
4 320km
5 660km
6 110km

Activity D

Round off these distances to the nearest thousand kilometres.

Answer like this: 1 = *4000*km

1 3860km
2 6420km
3 2950km
4 4100km
5 7003km
6 1507km

Look at this map of Brazil. It shows the main cities in Brazil.

There are some big cities in Brazil, but there are also large areas of Brazil that have no cities at all.

The largest cities in Brazil are along the coast. It is easier to move goods in and out of Brazil by sea.

The roads to the areas in the centre of Brazil are not very good.

The city of Brasilia was built away from the coast to try and open up this part of Brazil for more settlement.

In the rain forest most of the settlements are next to the big rivers. Building roads through the rain forest can destroy the land.

Figure 2

Activity E

Copy and complete these sentences.

1. Brazil has (no / some) large cities.
2. The largest cities in Brazil are (along the coast / in the rain forest).
3. In the rain forest the largest settlements are near (rivers / mountains).
4. The roads in Brazil are usually very (poor / good).
5. Brasilia is a city built (inland / on the coast).

Activity F

Look at Figure 2. Use the scale line to measure the distances below to the nearest **hundred** kilometres.

Answer like this: 1 = 400km

1. From São Paulo to Rio de Janeiro.
2. From Brasilia to Rio de Janeiro.
3. From Manaus to Belem.
4. From Recife to Brasilia.
5. From São Paulo to Porto Alegre.
6. From Boa Vista to Porto Alegre.
7. From Rio Branco to Recife.

Activity G

Look at Figure 1. Use the scale line to measure the distances between the cities below, to the nearest **thousand** kilometres.

Answer like this: 1 = 8000km

1. From Rio de Janeiro to London.
2. From Rome to London.
3. From São Paulo to Rome.
4. From London to New York.
5. From London to Sydney.
6. From London to Tokyo.

Activity H

Look at Figure 2 and measure the distances from Brasilia to six other cities in Brazil, to the nearest hundred kilometres. (Do not use the cities in Activity F.)

Activity I

Write three sentences about what you have found by measuring the distances between Brazil's cities.

Towns and Cities in Italy

- Rivers, railways and roads are not all straight.

How can we measure their length?

This section is about towns and cities in Italy.

Italy has some very old towns and cities. Like towns and cities all over the world, those in Italy are linked together by roads, rivers and railways.

So, measuring the distance between towns and cities in a straight line can give a false picture. Sometimes you may need to measure a distance which is not a straight line. Look at the river in Figure 1. It links the towns shown as A and D. The lines in Figure 2 are almost the same shape.

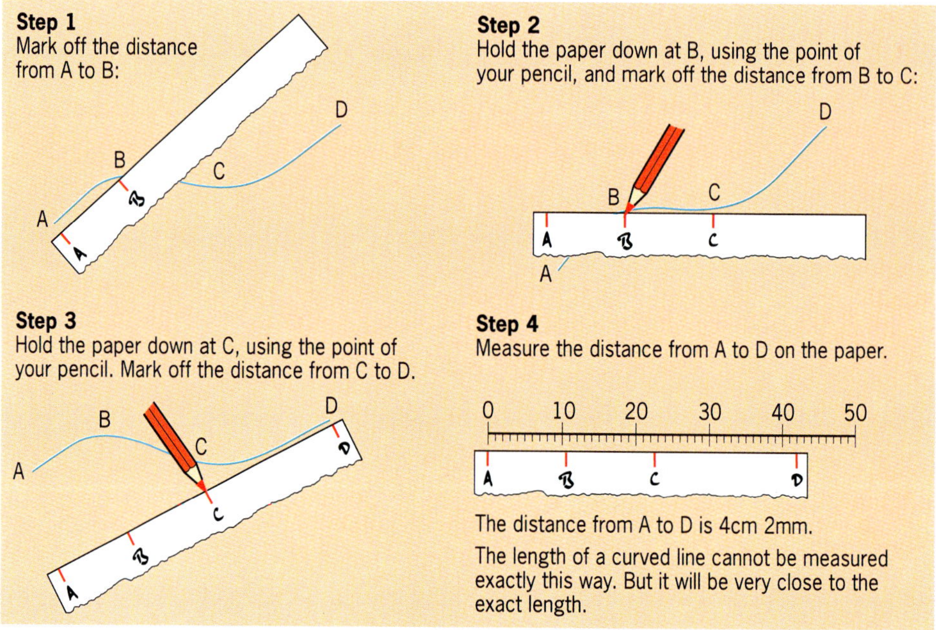

Figure 3

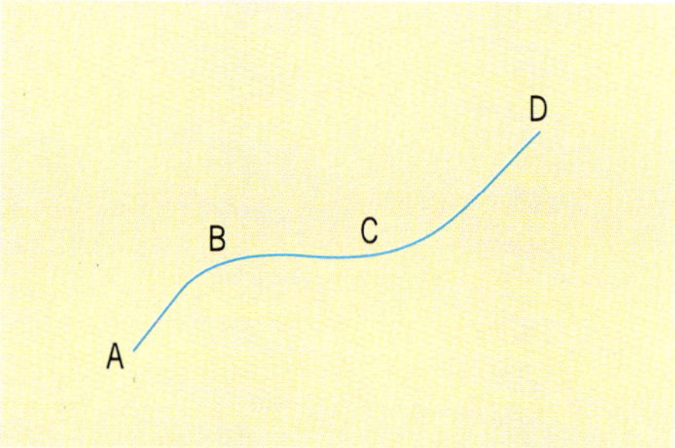

Figure 1

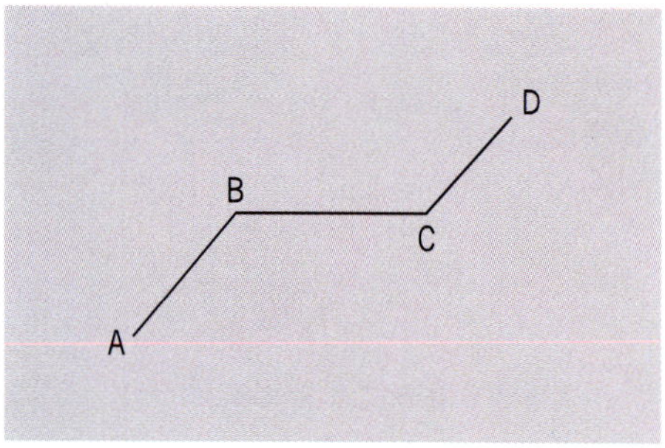

Figure 2

In Figure 2 the lines from A to B, from B to C and from C to D can be measured. When they are added together they will show the real distance between the towns A and D. The curved line in Figure 1 can also be measured in the way shown in Figure 3.

Activity A

Measure the real lengths of these rivers using the scale line.

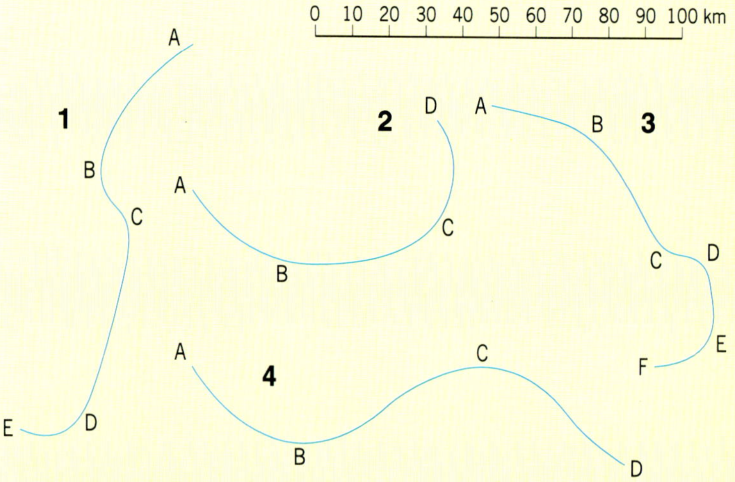

Activity B

1 Measure the distances in a straight line between the places shown in Activity A.

2 What is the difference between the straight line distances and the distances measured along the curves?

The shape of the land can be a problem when linking towns and cities together. The shape of the land is called the **relief**.

In Italy there are many mountains. There are the Alps in the North and the Apennines running down the centre of the country.

Look at this map of Italy. It shows most of the big towns and cities. The biggest cities are Milan, Turin, Genoa, Rome, Naples and Palermo.

The area between Turin, Milan and Genoa is very important for industry. This industry includes car making, shipbuilding and oil refining. These cities are also important to the farming areas all around.

Venice, Florence and Rome are very old cities. Many tourists visit them.

In the South of Italy, Naples is very important. It is not as well developed as cities in the North.

Roads have been built to try and link the North and the South. But the relief makes it difficult.

Figure 4 Italy

Activity C

Copy and complete the sentences below.

1 The shape of the land is called (relief / reveal).
2 The biggest cities in Italy are in the (North / South).
3 The South has (no / some) big cities.
4 The biggest cities are Milan, Turin, Genoa, Naples, Palermo and (Rome / Florence).
5 Florence, Rome and Venice are (old / new) cities.
6 The most important area for industry is between Turin, Genoa and (Naples / Milan).

Activity D

Use Figure 4 and copy and complete these sentences. Measure the distances in a straight line.

1 It is _____ km from Genoa to Florence.
2 It is _____ km from Rome to Naples.
3 It is _____ km from Milan to Venice.
4 It is _____ km from Turin to Florence.
5 It is _____ km from Naples to Venice.
6 It is _____ km from Milan to Rome.

Activity E

Do Activity D again, but this time measure the distances by road.

Activity F

Use Figure 4 to measure these distances.

1 The length of the River Po.
2 The distance along the coast from Genoa to Reggio.
3 The distance around the coast of Sicily.

The Growth of Cities in the UK

- Why are some towns and cities bigger than others?

Let's see how places grow.

This section is about the growth of cities and towns in the UK.

The place where a settlement starts to grow is called its **site**. A long time ago settlements grew around many different sites. Figure 1 shows some of them.

Many towns and cities grew up because of industry which started to develop on Britain's coalfields. These were **industrial towns**. They were the centre for factories and the homes of the people who worked there. Industry in these towns included iron and steel, textiles and shipbuilding.

Some of the largest towns and cities grew up where a river meets the sea. These settlements are **ports**, like Liverpool, Glasgow and London.

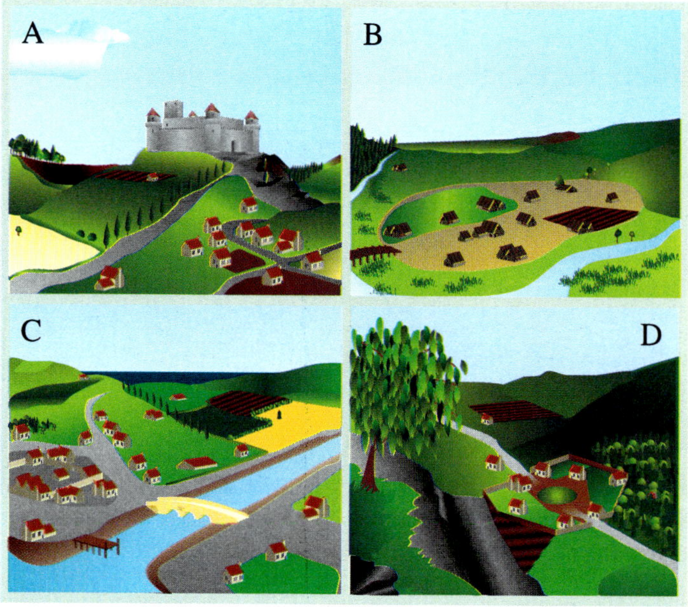

Figure 1

Figure 2 UK cities

Activity A

Look at Figure 1 and match the letters with these sites.

Answer like this: A = Defence site.

Dry site	Defence site	Gap site	Crossing site

Activity B

Copy and complete these sentences.

1 The place where a settlement starts to grow is called its (industry / site).

2 A lot of settlements start to grow because of (industry / site).

Activity C

Look at Figure 2.

1 Name five cities near the coalfields.

2 Name five cities that are ports.

3 Name five other cities.

The largest city in the UK is London. More than eight million people live in London. This is more than in the whole of some countries.

London was an early settlement site at a crossing of the River Thames. Many years ago the Romans built their settlement on higher ground above the river. They called this settlement Londinium.

The river site saw London grow as a **port** and it also started to grow as a **centre for business**. There are a great many banks and offices in London. These are the service industries.

The location of London also helped it to grow as an **industrial city**. The things needed for industry in factories were not far away. These are secondary industries. London also has good transport links with other parts of the country. So the things it does not have can be transported there by road and rail.

London has two very large airports. Tourists from all over the world visit London for holidays. It is a **tourist city**.

Look at the chart (Figure 3). It shows the distances between cities, in a straight line. The distance between London and Birmingham is 170km. The distance between Northampton and Oxford is 55km. This chart is called a **distance matrix**.

Figure 3

	Oxford	Northampton	Cambridge	Birmingham	London
Oxford					
Northampton	55				
Cambridge					
Birmingham		75			
London	85			170	

Activity D

Name five reasons why London grew to be a very large city.

Activity E

Copy and complete the distance matrix (Figure 3) by measuring the distances between the cities shown on the map in Figure 4.

Figure 4

Activity F

Measure these distances by road.

1 London to Reading.
2 London to Southampton.
3 London to Coventry.
4 London to Leicester.
5 London to Swindon.
6 London to Folkestone.

Activity G

Make up your own distance matrix for five different cities shown in Figure 4.

Activity H

Which way does a city grow? Like A, or like B? Write three sentences to explain your answer.

The Height of the Land

- A map is flat, so how can it show the height of the land?

This section will show you how.

This section is about showing hills and mountains on a map.

Look at the simple map of a hill in Figure 1. It uses colour to show the height of the land. The letter X shows a place more than 400 metres high. The same map can be drawn without a map key. Figure 2 also shows this hill, but does not need a map key.

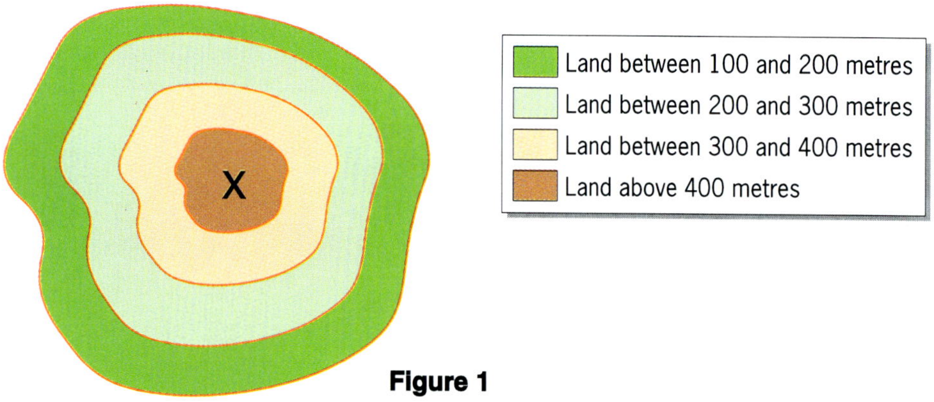

Figure 1

When the colour is taken away, the map looks like Figure 3. The lines look like a plan of paths at the same height.

The lines are called **contours**. A contour is a line on a map that joins all the places of the same height.

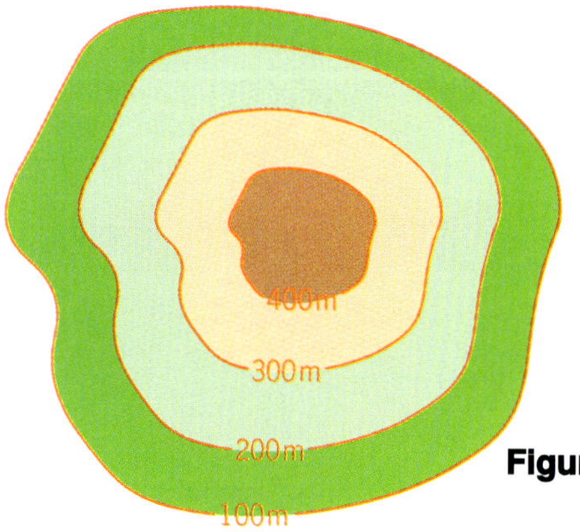

Figure 2

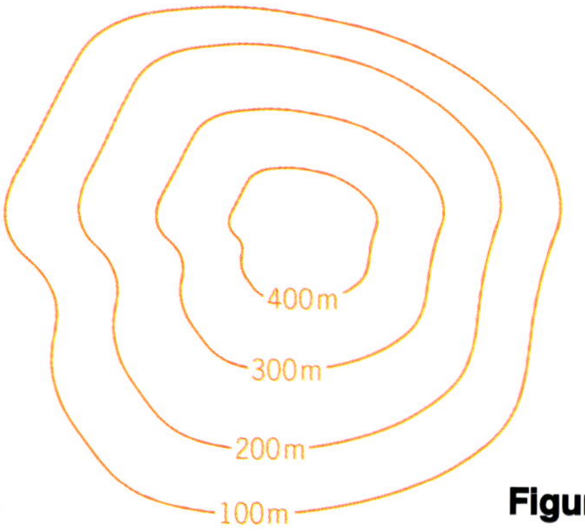

Figure 3

Activity A

Look at Figure 1, and then match the letters on the map below with these heights.

1. Land between 100 and 200 metres.
2. Land between 200 and 300 metres.
3. Land between 300 and 400 metres.
4. Land above 400 metres.

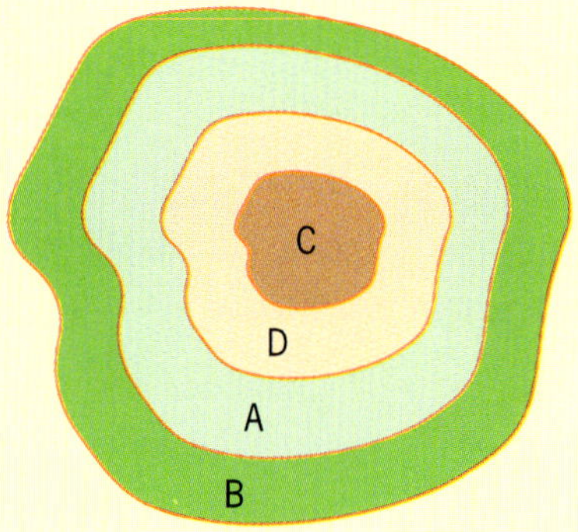

Activity B

Match the letters on the map below with these heights.

1. Land between 100 and 200 metres.
2. Land between 200 and 300 metres.
3. Land between 300 and 400 metres.
4. Land above 400 metres.

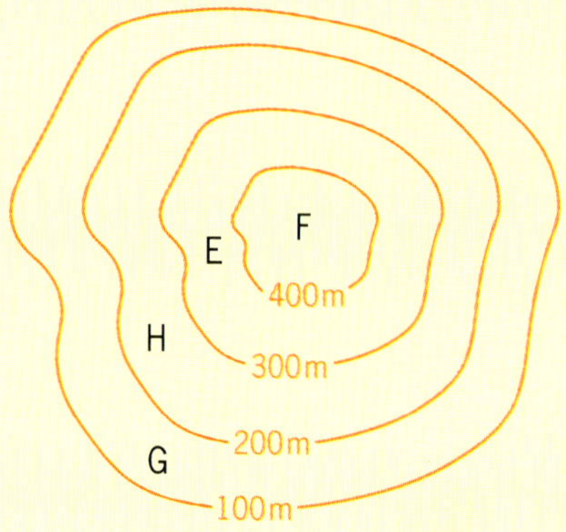

If the contours are close together, it means the slope is steep:

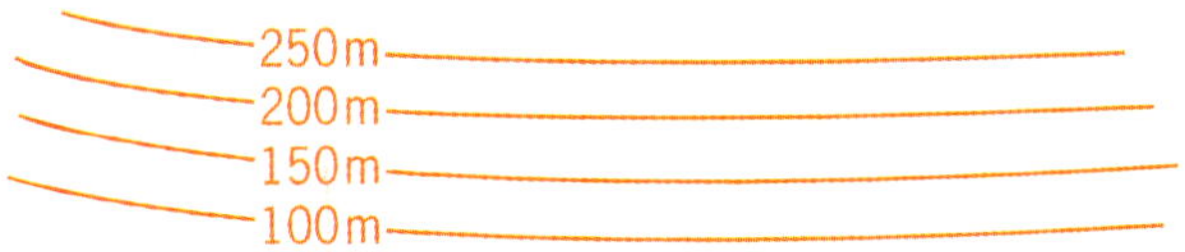

If the contours are far apart, it means the slope is gentle:

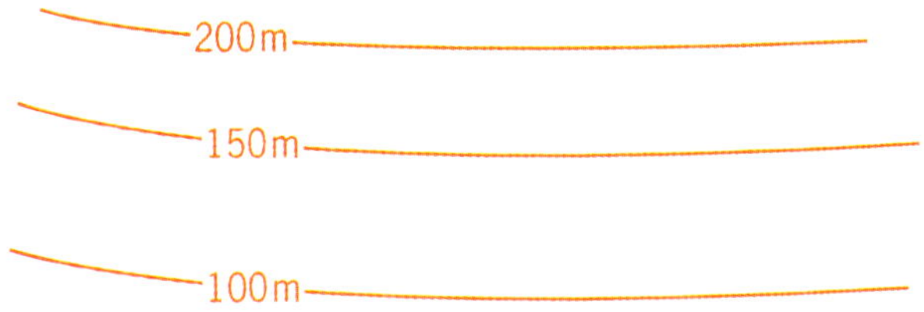

Look at this simple map or plan of a hill (Figure 4). A path over the hill shows the places A to H. A is at 100 metres, B is at 200 metres, C is at 300 metres and so on.

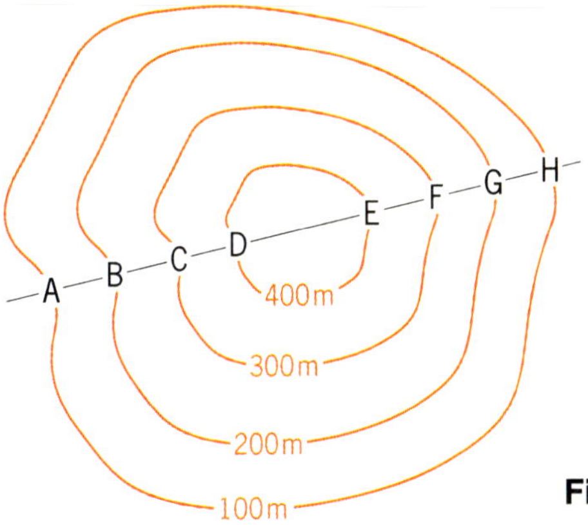

Figure 4

This is what a **section** of the hill looks like, along the line from A to H (Figure 5). A is 100 metres above the sea, B is 200 metres above the sea and so on.

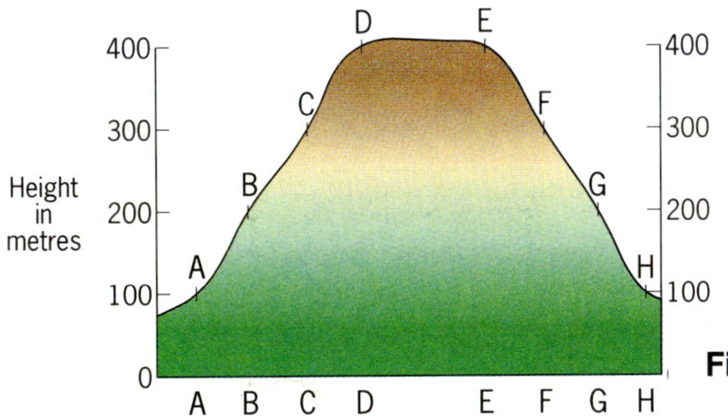

Figure 5

Activity C

Copy and complete these sentences.

1 A line on a map joining points of the same height is called a (contour / cone).
2 Contours close together show a (steep / gentle) slope.
3 Contours far apart make a (steep / gentle) slope.

Activity D

1 Copy this pattern of contours.
2 Is this a steep slope or a gentle slope?

Activity E

Draw a contour pattern for a gentle slope.

Activity F

1 Copy this contour pattern of Windy Hill.
2 Colour in red the land above 500 metres.
3 What is the height of Y?
4 Write STEEP on the steep slope.
5 Write GENTLE on the gentle slope.
6 Colour in green the land below 200 metres.
7 What is the height of X?

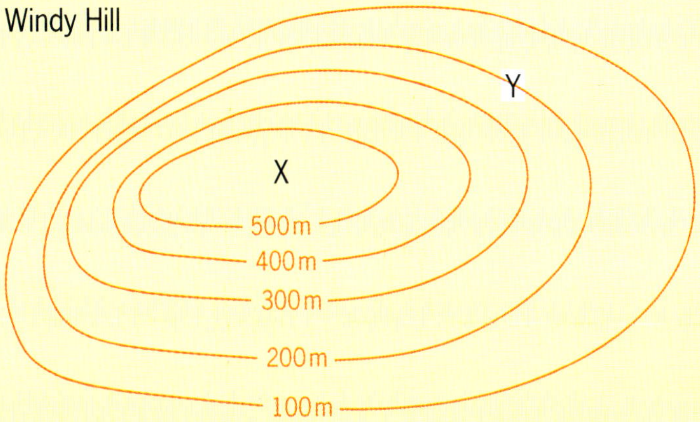

The UK's Hills and Mountains

- The hills and mountains of the UK are wetter than the lowlands.

Let's take a look at them.

This section is about hills and mountains in the UK.

Look at this OS map of part of the Lake District.

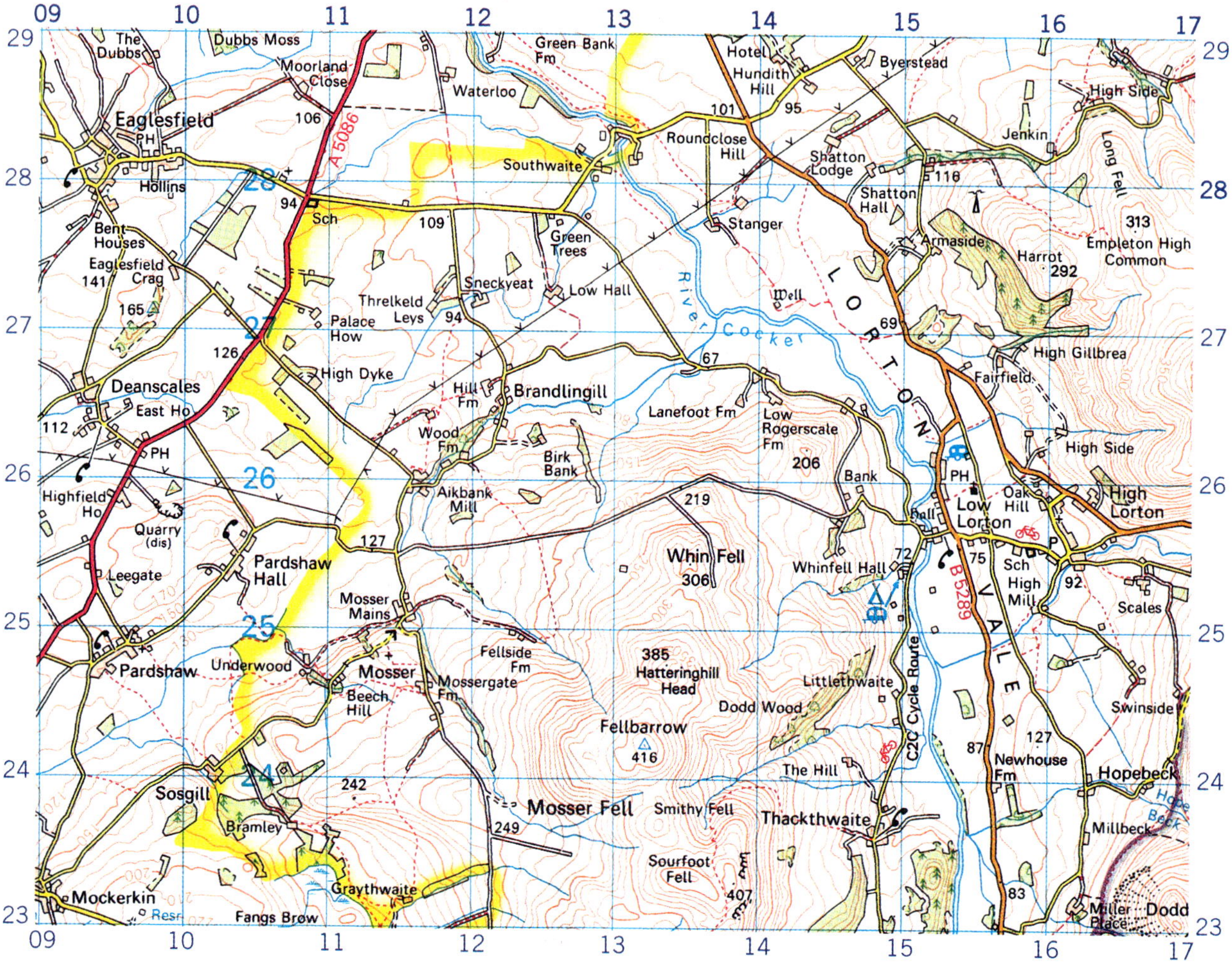

Figure 1

Activity A

Write down if you think the land is gentle or steep in the following grid squares.

Answer like this: 1 1324 – steep

1 1324	**3** 1524	**5** 1127	**7** 1424
2 1626	**4** 1628	**6** 1224	**8** 1325

Activity B

Write down any two contour heights named in these grid squares.

1 1325	**3** 1326	**5** 0925
2 1626	**4** 0923	

Activity C

1. Write down five heights shown along the B5289 road.
2. Write down three heights shown along the A5086 road.
3. Write down the highest point shown on the map.
4. Name the highest point on the map.

Activity D

1. Write down the height of the land at these points.

a 113255	**c** 138232	**e** 135259	**g** 151281
b 112238	**d** 159242	**f** 098271	**h** 136268

2. Write down five six-figure references of your own to show the height of the land.

There are no large cities in the highlands of the UK. It is more difficult to build roads, so the settlements are not linked together as well as they are in the lowlands.

In the UK, the mountains are colder in winter than the lowlands. The temperature of the air gets lower as the height of the land gets higher. So in winter, the roads of the UK's mountains may be blocked with snow.

The mountains also have more rain. Look at Figure 2. It is a section across some mountains in the UK. The relief of the land makes the air rise. As it rises it gets colder. Rain-drops form and there are more clouds. So it rains. Rain made this way is called **relief rainfall**.

One side of the mountains gets more rain than the other. The side with less rain is called the **rain shadow**.

Figure 2

In the UK most of the rain shadow areas are to the east of the mountains. This is because most of the wet winds come from the west.

The soil in the highlands is not as good as the soil in the lowlands. A lot of the goodness is washed out by the rain.

Activity E

1 Match the letters on the diagram below with these words.

Answer like this: A = Mountains

Rain shadow	Mountains	Rain
Clouds	Relief rainfall	West

2 Copy this diagram and label it correctly.

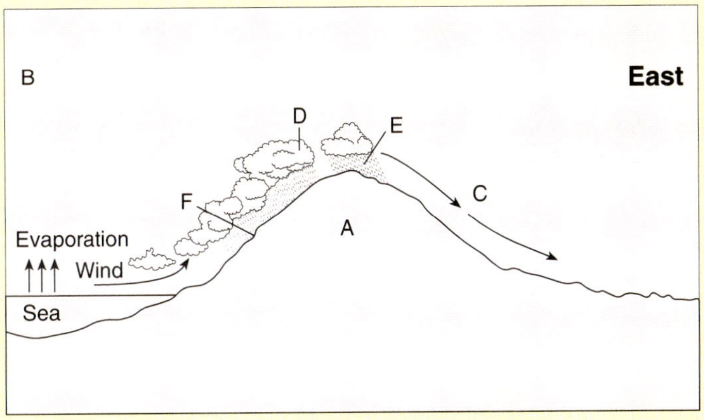

Activity F

Copy and complete these sentences.

1 The best roads are in the (highlands / lowlands).
2 The coldest parts of the UK are the (highlands / lowlands).
3 Most towns and cities are in the (highlands / lowlands).
4 The best soils are in the (highlands / lowlands).
5 Most of the rain falls in the (highlands / lowlands).
6 The shape of the land makes the air rise in the (highlands / lowlands).

Activity G

1 Name the mountains nearest to your home.
2 Write five sentences about living in the mountains.

The Mountains of Europe

- The geography of the mountains is different to the geography of the lowlands.

Let's see why.

This section is about mountains in Europe.

Mountains are made over a very long period of time. These drawings show how this can happen.

Stage 1

A very long time ago layers of rock were made at the bottom of lakes and seas. These rocks are called **sedimentary rocks**. The layers of rock are called **strata**.

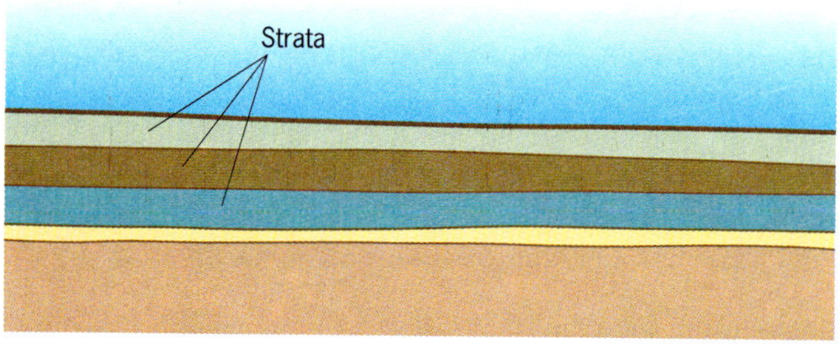

Stage 2

The strata were folded up. The high parts are called **anticlines**. The low parts are called **synclines**.

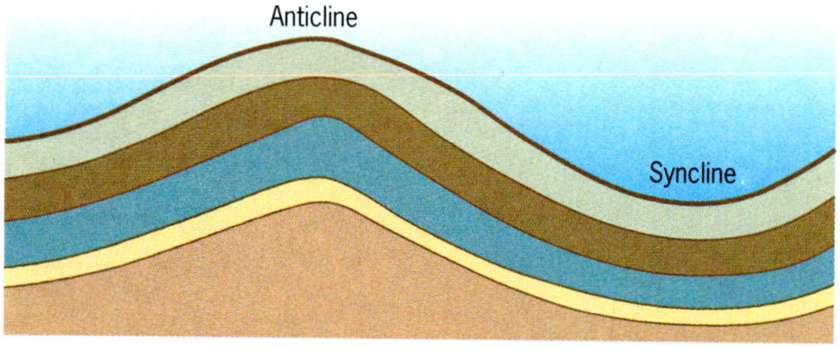

Stage 3

The shape of the land was changed by rivers, ice and the weather. This is called **erosion**. The anticlines were made into mountains and the synclines were made into low land.

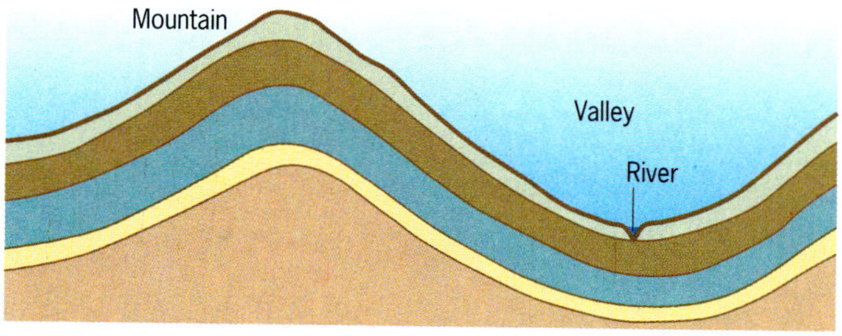

Mountains made in this way are called **fold mountains**. Not all mountains are fold mountains.

Some mountains were made where there were large cracks called **faults**. Some of the strata were forced up along these faults. These are sometimes called **block mountains**.

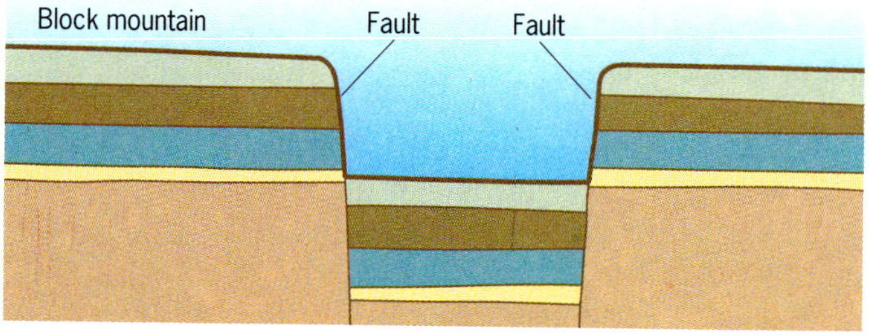

Activity A

Match the words below with their meanings.

Anticline	Syncline	Erosion
Fault	Strata	

■ – changing the shape of the land by water and ice.
■ – a large crack in the rocks.
■ – layers of rock.
■ – the high parts of mountain folds.
■ – the low parts of mountain folds.

Activity B

Look at Stage 1 and write down three sentences to explain how sedimentary rocks are made.

Activity C

1 Write down two ways that block mountains and fold mountains are alike.

2 Write down two ways that block mountains and fold mountains are different.

On a lot of maps the mountains are shown by dark colours. The colours show places of the same height. They are like a plan of the mountains.

A line of mountains is called a **mountain range**.

Look at this map of the mountain ranges in Europe. The fold mountains are very high. They are much higher than the mountains in the UK. This means they are much colder in winter.

The Alps are part of the highest mountain range in Europe. The Apennines in Italy were made at about the same time as the Alps. They are part of the **Alpine** fold mountains. The Alps are covered in snow in the winter. Many tourists go to the Alps for skiing holidays.

In Italy the Alps run from west to east, but the Apennines run from north to south. The direction of the slope is also important. This is called the **aspect**. Some slopes face the sun, but others do not get a lot of sun. Sunshine is important in farming.

Most of the large rivers in Europe start in the mountains. This is their **source**.

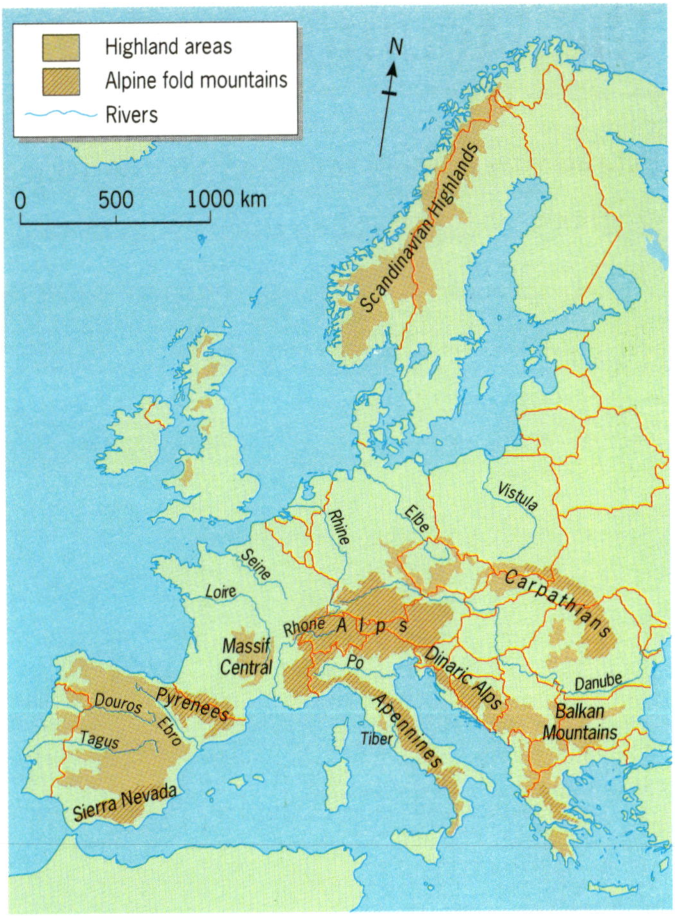

Figure 5

Activity D

Copy and complete these sentences.

1. A line of mountains is called a (hill / range).
2. The Alps are much (higher / lower) than the mountains in the UK.
3. The direction of the slope is called the (Alps / aspect).
4. The (sauce / source) of many rivers is in the mountains.
5. The Alps run from east to (east / west).

Activity E

Look at Figure 5.

1. Name five mountain ranges that were made at the same time as the Alps.
2. Name three rivers which have their source in the Alps.

Activity F

Look at Photograph 1 and write five sentences about what you think it is like to live in the Alps.

Activity G

1. Draw a sketch of the Alps in Photograph 1.
2. Label your sketch with the words below.

Snow on upper slopes		Steep sides	
Farm building	Valley	Forest	Grassland

Photograph 1

The Mountains of the World

- Where are the world's highest mountains?

Let's take a look at a map to find out.

This section is about the mountains of the world.

Look at this map. It shows the main mountain ranges in the world.

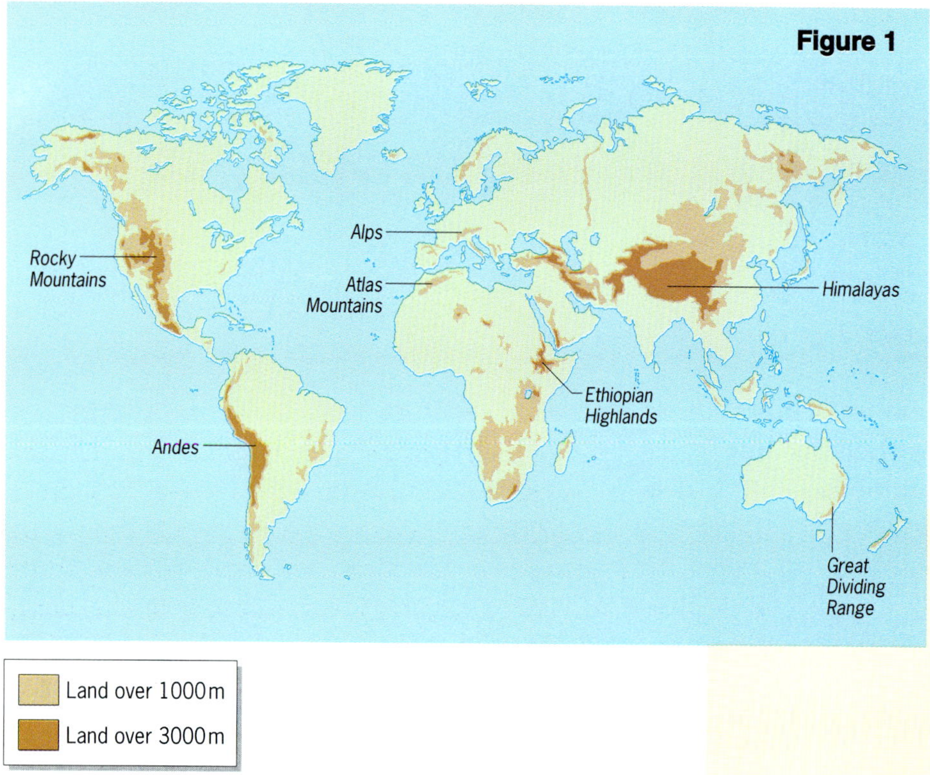

Photograph 1 The Andes

All over the world, life in the mountains is different to life in the lowlands. In the mountains most of the settlements are small, and cut off from the larger towns and cities because it is difficult to build good roads. There may be some mining in the mountains, but there is not much secondary industry and this means fewer jobs.

Farming can be difficult because the steep slopes do not make it easy to use machines.

Temperatures fall with **altitude**, or height of the land. Where the winds come from the sea, the mountains will have a great deal of rain. If the woodland is cut down there may be some soil erosion. Where the winds do not come from the sea, the mountains may be dry areas with rocky soils.

Activity A

Look at Photograph 1.

1 Write a sentence about the mountains in Photograph 1.
2 Write a sentence about the lowland in Photograph 1.

Activity B

Look at Figure 1.

1 Name the mountains over 3000 metres above sea level.
2 Name the mountains over 1000 metres above sea level.
3 Name a mountain range in South America.
4 Name a mountain range in North America.
5 Name a mountain range in Africa.
6 Name a mountain range in Australia.

In most mountain areas there is a change in the use of the land, as the altitude also changes. Figure 2 tries to show this pattern. The height where the land use changes may be different in different mountain ranges. There may be snow on the top of the mountains.

The population of mountain areas is falling in most parts of the world. Many people leave the small settlements to look for work in the cities. Many young people do not like the way of life in the mountain areas.

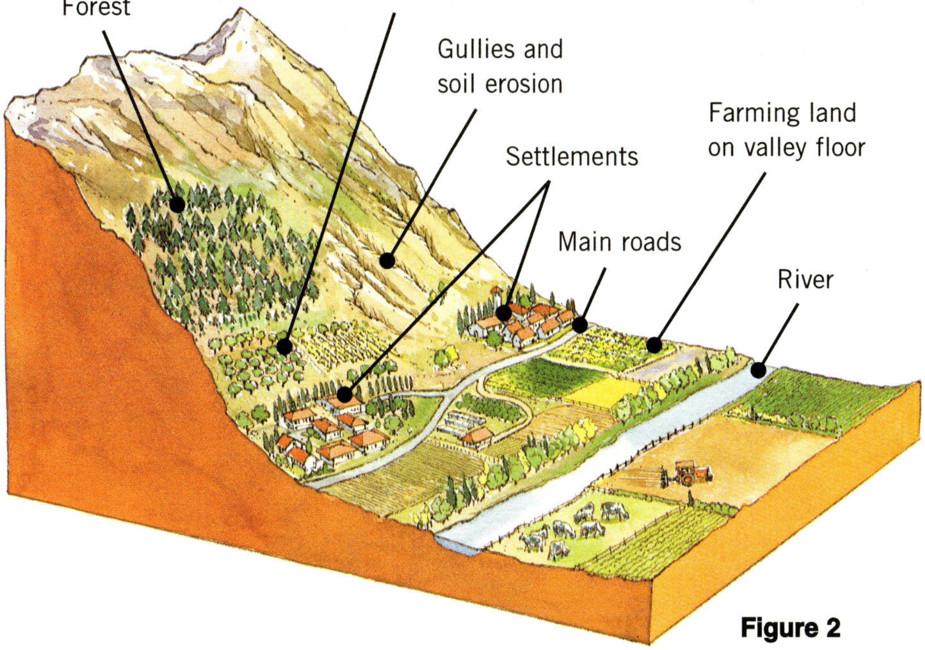

Figure 2

This movement from the countryside to the cities is called **rural depopulation**. One part of Europe which has seen a lot of rural depopulation is the Apennines and the mountain farms of the south of Italy. This is a poor farming area. In the past, many families have moved from the south of Italy to the USA to start a new life. Most of them moved between the years 1870 and 1914, to live in big cities like New York.

A person who goes to live in another part of the country is called a **migrant**. People who go to live in a new country are called **immigrants**. Moving from one country to another is called **emigration**.

Activity C

Look at Figure 2 and Photograph 2.

1 Write down three things you can see in both Figure 2 and Photograph 2.

2 Draw a labelled sketch of Photograph 2.

Activity D

Match these words with their meaning below.

Soil erosion	Altitude	Rural depopulation
Emigration	Migrant	Immigrant

- ■ – people moving away from farming areas to live in the towns.
- ■ – the height of the land.
- ■ – when the soil is washed away.
- ■ – a person who moves to another part of the country.
- ■ – when people go to live in a new country.
- ■ – people who live in a new country.

Activity E

If you were living in the South of Italy, what would you think about living in a village in the Apennines? Write five sentences.

Photograph 2 The Apennines

The Climate of the UK 1

- What is the difference between weather and climate?

Let's measure them to find out.

This section is about how graphs are used to show climate.

A graph is a special kind of diagram. It shows how two things are related. Look at this bar graph.

The bar graph shows the amount of rainfall at Fort William in Scotland for one year. It shows how rainfall and time are related.

The information needed to draw a graph is called **data**.

How to draw a bar graph

Step 1
A bar graph is drawn inside a frame. The line going across the page is called the horizontal axis. The line going up the page is called the vertical axis.

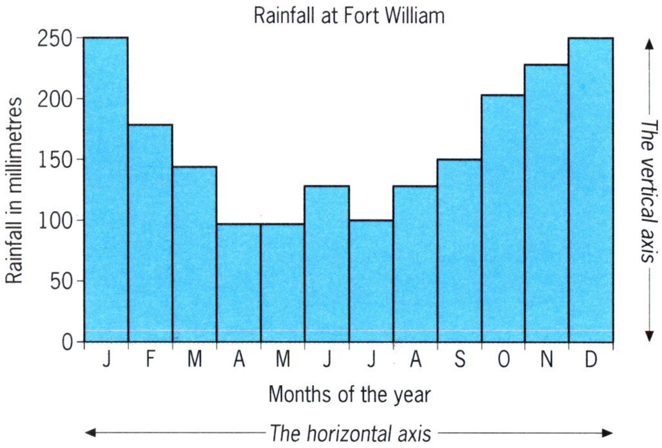

Figure 1

Step 2
Look at the data. Figure 2 gives the rainfall data for the city of Norwich.

Months of the year	J	F	M	A	M	J	J	A	S	O	N	D
Rainfall in millimetres	58	46	37	39	48	39	63	56	54	61	64	53

Figure 2

Step 3
Draw the horizontal axis to show the months of the year.

Draw the vertical axis to show the rainfall.

Make sure the scale along each axis is a good fit on your page.

Activity A

Copy and complete this bar graph of rainfall in Norwich.

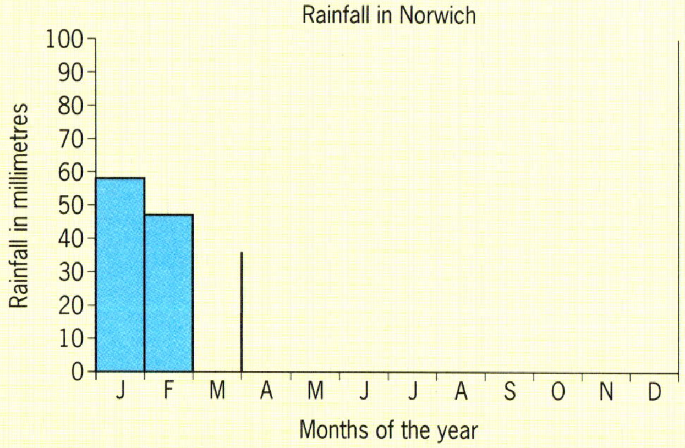

Activity B

Look at the bar graph of rainfall in Fort William (Figure 1). Write down how much rain there is in these months.

Answer like this: 1 January 250mm

1 January
2 July
3 December
4 May
5 September
6 March

Step 4
Label the horizontal axis and the vertical axis.

Give the graph a title.

Draw the bars to show the rainfall.

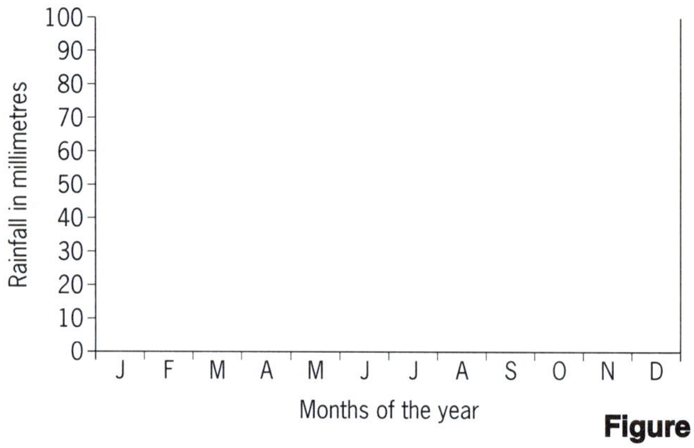

Figure 3

The amount of rainfall is measured by a rain gauge. A rain gauge is placed in an open space on the ground.

The rain runs into a funnel and then into a jar. Rainfall is measured every day using a measuring cylinder. It is measured in millimetres.

There will be some changes in the amount of rainfall from year to year. The data shows how much rain falls in a place for most of the time.

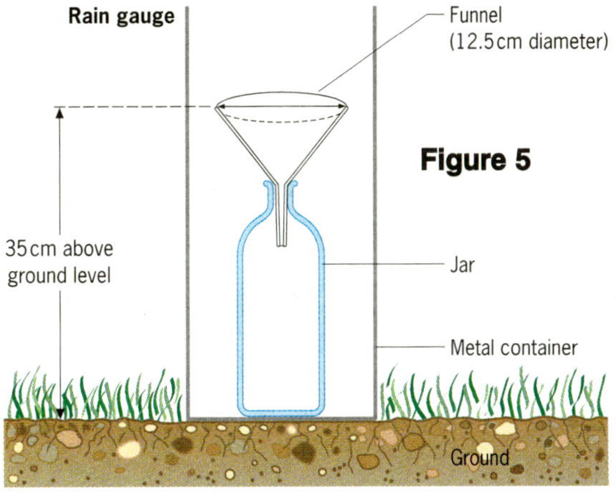

Figure 5

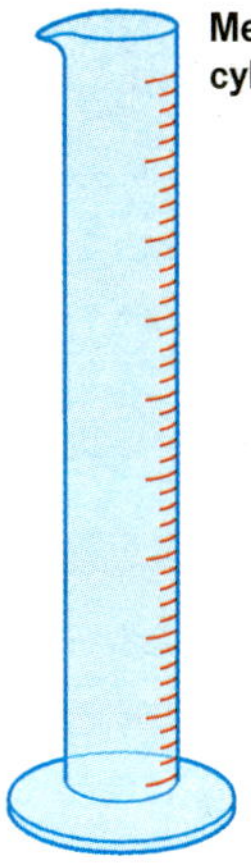

Figure 6

The rain gauge measures the **weather**. The bar graph shows the **climate** over a long period of time.

Most of the rain in the UK falls in the west. This is because most of the winds over the UK come from the west (Figure 7). They have blown over the Atlantic Ocean and are wet winds.

Depression rainfall is blown in from the Atlantic Ocean.

Relief rainfall is also heavy in the west because most of the hills and mountains in the UK are in the west.

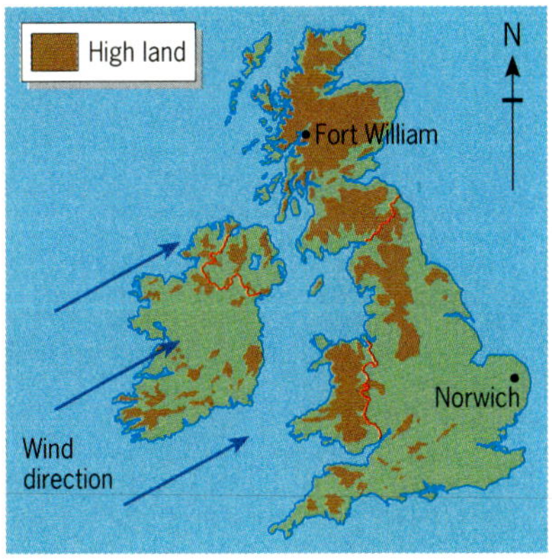

Figure 7

Activity C

Look at Figure 1.

1 Name the wettest month.
2 Name the driest month.
3 Which month had 170 millimetres of rain?
4 Which month had 210 millimetres of rain?
5 Which months had less than 100 millimetres of rain?
6 Which months had more than 200 millimetres of rain?

Activity D

1 What is the total amount of rainfall in Fort William?
2 What is the total amount of rainfall in Norwich?
3 Which place has the higher rainfall, Norwich or Fort William?

Activity E

Copy and complete these sentences.

1 Fort William is in the (east / west) of the UK.
2 Norwich is in the (east / west) of the UK.
3 Most rain in the UK falls in the (east / west).

Activity F

Copy this drawing of a rain gauge. Label your drawing with the words below. (Use Figure 5 to help you.)

Jar	Metal container	Ground	Funnel

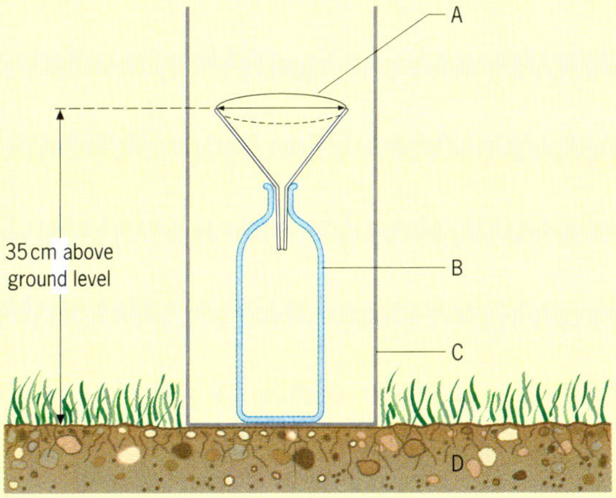

Activity G

Use the graphs and the diagrams to write five sentences about rainfall in the UK.

The Climate of the UK 2

- Is the UK's temperature the same all over the country?

Let's find out why it isn't.

This section is about how graphs are used to show temperature.

A line graph is used to show temperature. Look at the line graph in Figure 1. It shows the temperatures for the town of Falmouth in Cornwall.

The graph shows what the temperatures are like for most of the time. They are average temperatures.

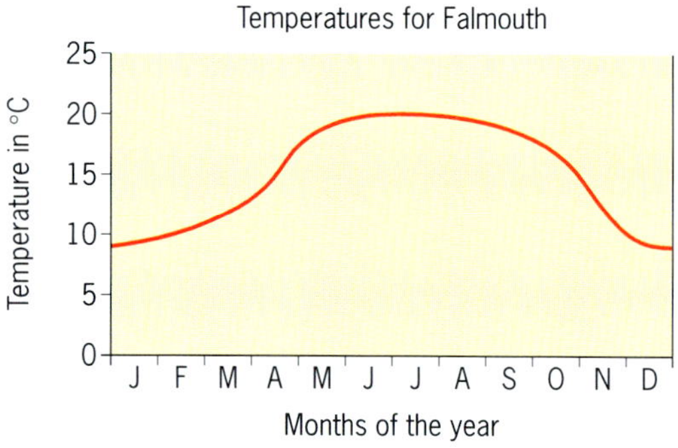

Figure 1

Activity A

Copy and complete the line graph of temperatures for Edinburgh.

Activity B

Look at Figure 1 and write down the temperatures for Falmouth at these times.

Answer like this: 1 January – 5°C.

1 January
2 July
3 December
4 May
5 September
6 August

Activity C

Look at Figure 1 and answer the questions below by naming the months.

Answer like this: 1 Name the coldest month – December.

1. Name the coldest month.
2. Name the hottest month.
3. Which month had a temperature of 15°C?
4. Which months had a temperature of 20°C?
5. Which months had a temperature between 5°C and 10°C?

How to draw a line graph

Step 1

Look at the data. Choose the scale of the horizontal axis and the vertical axis. The months of the year go along the horizontal axis.

This data shows the average temperatures for Edinburgh in Scotland.

Months of the year	J	F	M	A	M	J	J	A	S	O	N	D
Temperature in °C	5	6	7	11	14	16	18	17	15	12	9	6

Step 2

Mark the temperature of each month with a large dot. Put each dot above the centre of the space for the months.

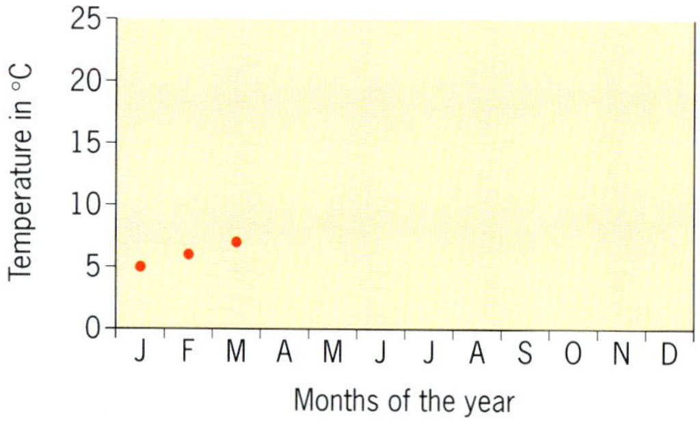

Step 3

Join the dots with a line and give the graph a title.

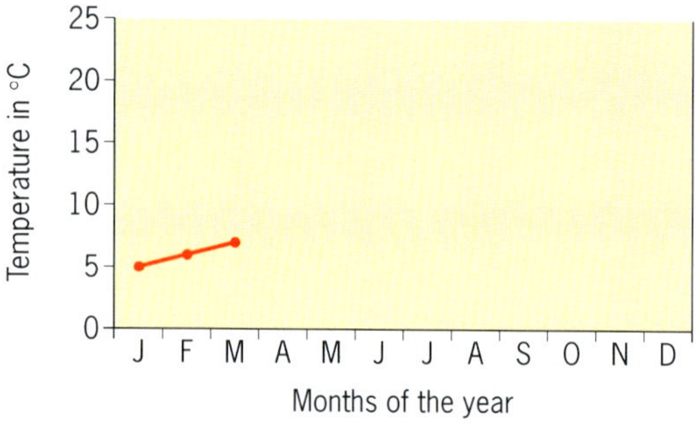

Temperature is measured by a **thermometer**. A **maximum** thermometer measures the highest temperatures. A **minimum** thermometer measures the lowest temperatures. The difference in temperature is called the **range**.

In summer the hottest parts of the country are in the south of the UK. This is because the north is further away from the equator than the south.

In winter the pattern is different. The winds come from the south-west and blow over the Atlantic Ocean. They cross a current of warm water called the North Atlantic Drift. This means the winds in the west of the UK are a little warmer. The east of the UK is further away from these winds, so it is colder.

The hills and mountains in the UK are colder than the rest of the country in both summer and winter.

Figure 5 shows the pattern of temperatures over the UK all year round.

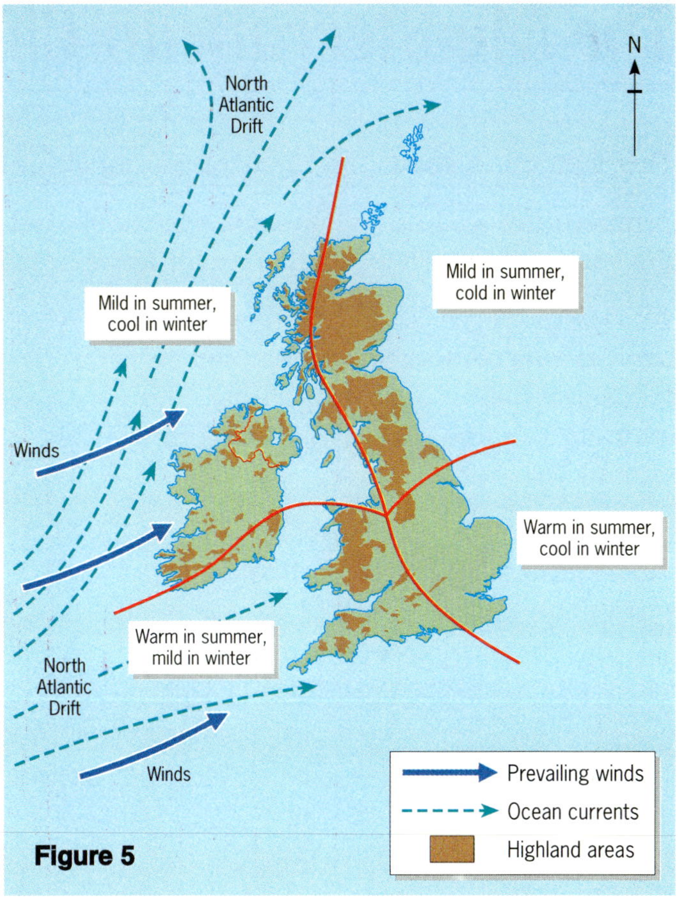

Figure 5

Activity D

Look at these thermometers. Write down the temperatures each one shows.

Answer like this: 1 = 5°C.

1

2

3

4

5 Which thermometer shows the maximum temperature?

6 Which thermometer shows the minimum temperature?

Activity E

Copy these sentences and then write True or False.

Answer like this: 1 Falmouth is warmer than Edinburgh in July. True

1 Falmouth is warmer than Edinburgh in July.

2 Edinburgh is colder than Falmouth in December.

3 Edinburgh is warmer than Falmouth in August.

4 Falmouth has a warmer summer than Edinburgh.

5 Edinburgh has a milder winter than Falmouth.

Activity F

Look at this map. Match the letters on the map with the words below.

- warm summers and cool winters
- mild summers and cool winters
- warm summers and mild winters
- mild summers and cool winters

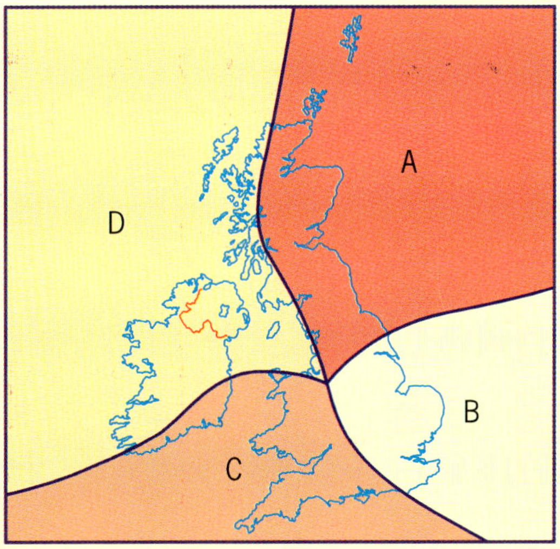

The Mediterranean Climate

- What happens when there is not enough rain?

The Mediterranean countries know what to do.

This section is about the Mediterranean climate.

Temperature and rainfall are sometimes shown on the same graph. This is called a **climograph**, because it shows the climate of a place.

Look at this climograph for Naples in the Mezzogiorno or South of Italy. The temperature line is drawn above the rainfall bar graph.

The left vertical axis shows the temperature. The right vertical axis shows the rainfall.

Figure 1

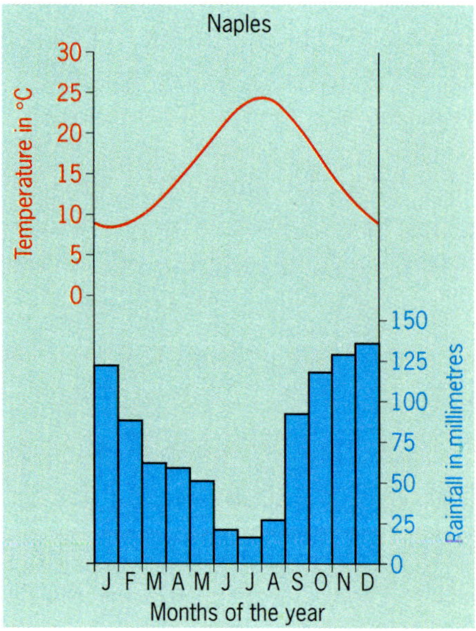

Figure 2

The South of Italy has a Mediterranean climate. The countries around the Mediterranean Sea have areas with this climate. But there are other parts of the world which also have a Mediterranean climate. Look at Figure 3.

Photograph 1 Naples

Activity A

Look at the climograph for Naples and answer these questions.

Answer like this: 1 24°C

1 What is the highest temperature?
2 What is the lowest temperature?
3 Which month has the highest temperature?
4 Which month has the lowest temperature?
5 Name any months without rainfall.
6 Name the four months with the most rainfall.

Activity B

Look at this data for Milan in Italy.

1 Use this data to draw a climograph, like the one in Figure 2.

Months of the year	J	F	M	A	M	J	J	A	S	O	N	D
Temperature in °C	0.5	3	8	12.5	17	21	23	22.5	19	12.5	7	2
Rainfall in millimetres	52	49	65	70	85	89	55	71	72	114	101	80

2 Use your climograph for Milan to write down six differences between the climates in the North and South of Italy.

The Mediterranean climate is located between latitudes 30° and 40°N, and 30° and 40°S (Figure 3). The areas are also on the west coasts of the continents.

In a Mediterranean climate the summers are always hot and dry. This is because the winds blow from the land to the sea for most of the time, so they do not bring rain.

In winter the winds blow from the sea to the land. These wet winds bring rain.

A long period of time without rain is called a **drought**. The summer drought in a Mediterranean climate causes problems for farmers. They need water for the land, but it may not rain for a very long time. Rivers and springs are used to water the land. This is called **irrigation**.

The sunny climate means that fruit grows very well. This includes **citrus fruits** like oranges, lemons and grapefruits, as well as other fruits such as grapes and peaches. Most of the world's fruit is grown in places with a Mediterranean climate, with the help of irrigation.

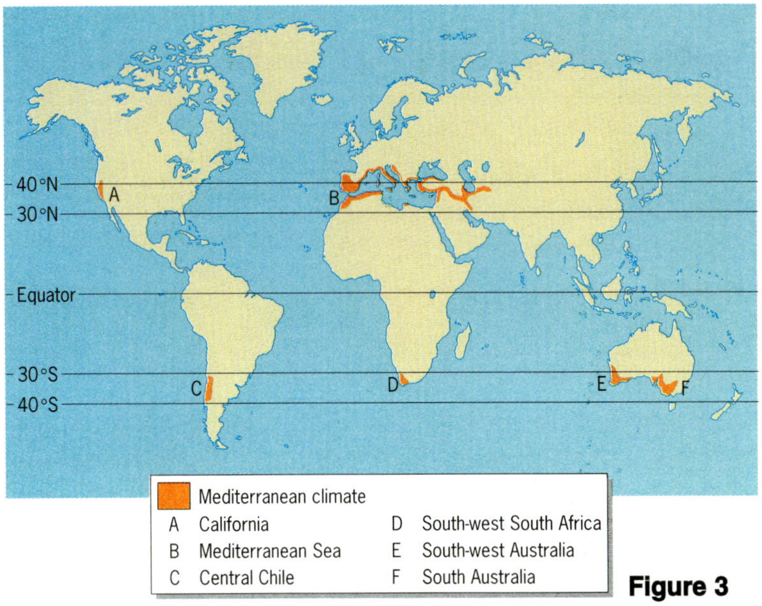

Figure 3

Photograph 2 Irrigating peaches

Activity C

Look at Figure 3 and name the areas in each continent which have a Mediterranean climate.

Answer like this: 1 North America = California.

Activity D

Name six fruits grown in a Mediterranean climate.

Activity E

Look at Photograph 2. Use the photograph to write five sentences about irrigation in a Mediterranean climate.

Activity F

Copy and complete these sentences.

1 The Mediterranean climates are on the (east / west) of the continents.

2 Mediterranean climates are between latitudes (30° and 40° / 40° and 50°).

Activity G

Match the words in the box with the meanings below.

Irrigation	Citrus	Drought	Spring	Olive

■ – a kind of fruit.
■ – a fruit important for its oil.
■ – water that comes from the ground.
■ – watering the land.
■ – a long time without rain.

Activity H

What do you think it would be like to live in a Mediterranean climate? Write six sentences or more to explain your answer.

The Climate of the Rain Forest

- Why is the rain forest so hot and wet?

The heat makes it rain.

This section is about the climate of the rain forest. It is called the equatorial climate.

The rain forest areas of the world are shown in Figure 1. They are all around the equator, so the climate is called the equatorial climate. Figure 2 shows the climograph for Manaus in the rain forest of Brazil.

A pie graph can show how the land is used. It is called a pie graph because each part looks like a piece from a pie. Look at these circles. They are all the same size. The names of the parts are written under the circles (Figure 3).

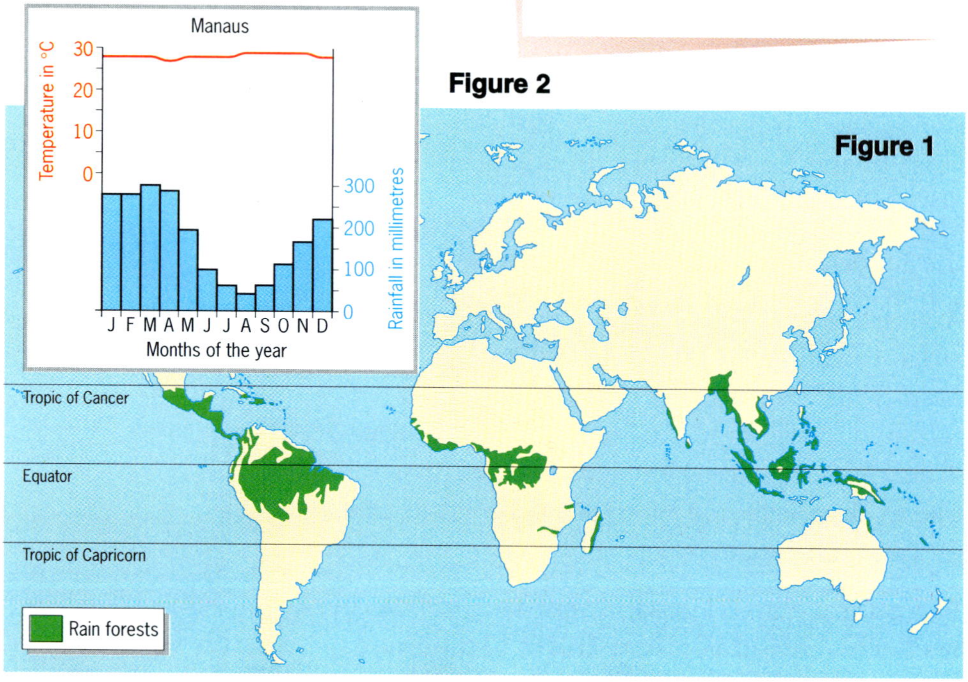

Figure 2

Figure 1

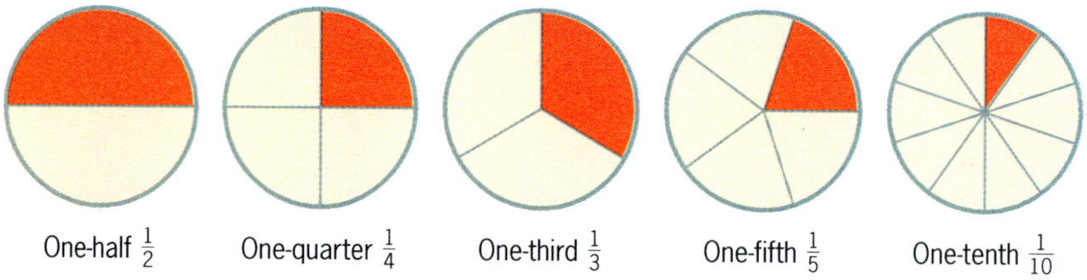

Figure 3

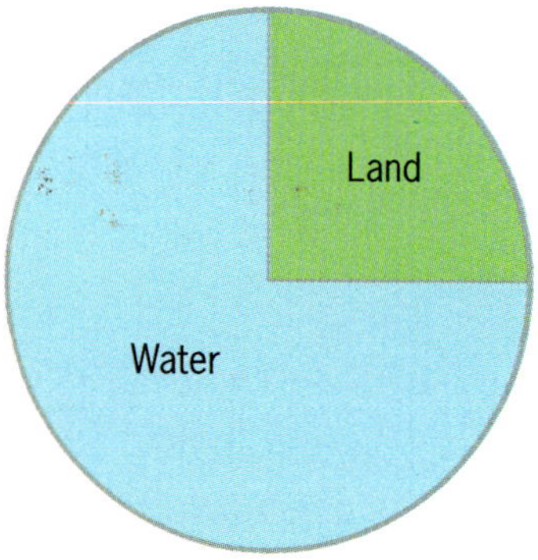

This pie graph shows how much of the world is land, and how much is water.

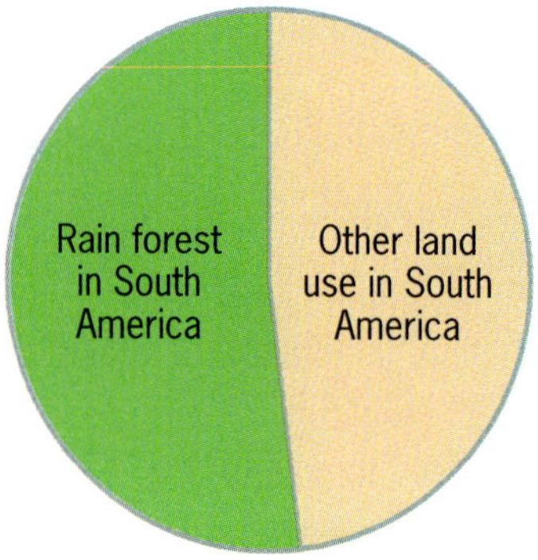

This pie graph shows how much of the land in South America is covered by rain forest.

Activity A

Look at these pie graphs and write down how much is in green.

Answer like this: 1 A quarter ($\frac{1}{4}$).

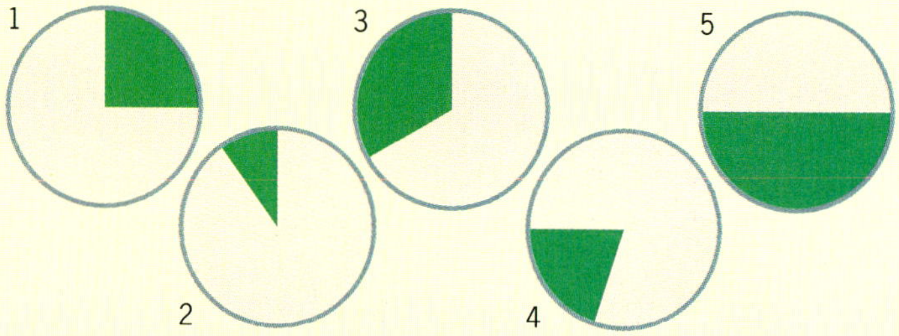

Activity B

1 How much of the world is water – $\frac{3}{4}$, $\frac{2}{5}$ or $\frac{1}{4}$?

2 How much of the world is land – $\frac{3}{4}$, $\frac{2}{3}$ or $\frac{1}{4}$?

3 How much of South America is rain forest – $\frac{1}{2}$, $\frac{1}{4}$ or $\frac{3}{4}$?

Look at the climograph of the rain forest at Manaus. It shows what an equatorial climate is like.

1 It is always hot, so there is no winter.
2 It is always wet.

There are some things about the equatorial climate that the climograph does not show.

1 There is very little wind.
2 There is a lot of cloud.
3 It is hot every day.
4 The heavy rain falls mostly in the afternoons.
5 The rain falls during heavy storms. There is much thunder and lightening.

The rainfall in an equatorial climate is called **convectional rainfall**. Every morning the rain forest begins to get hot.

By the middle of the day it is very hot. The hot air rises and the clouds build up. The clouds grow in size and turn very dark.

In the afternoon the air cools as it rises. The rain forms as the air cools. A storms begins and may last for about two hours.

It stays clear in the night.

Photograph 1

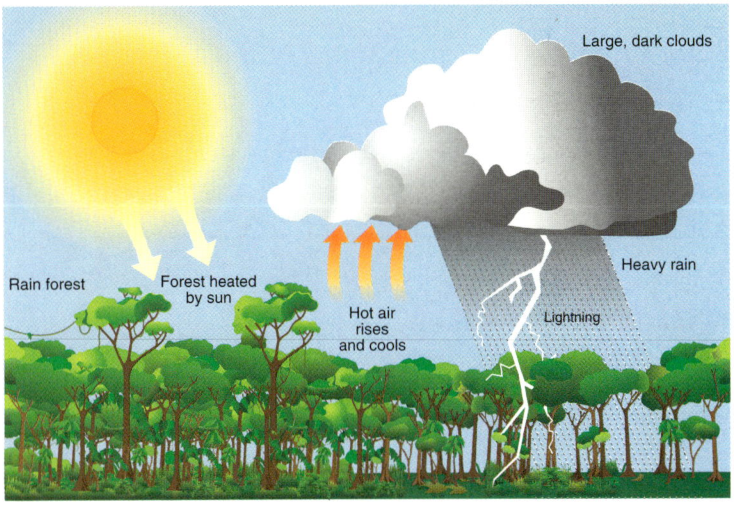

Figure 4 Convectional rainfall

Activity C

Look at this pie graph of land use in Brazil. How much of Brazil is rain forest? Is it one-quarter, one-half or three-quarters?

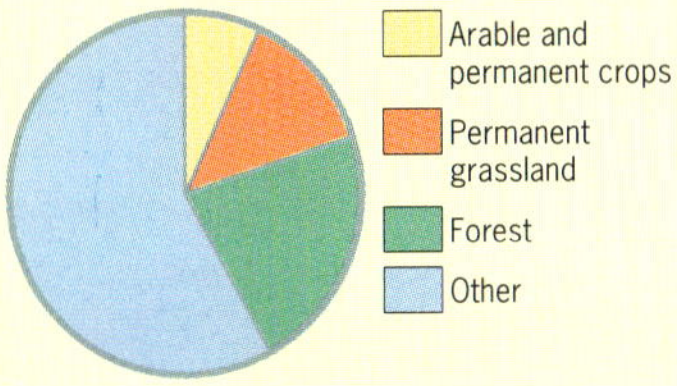

Activity D

Match the letters on this clock with the words below.

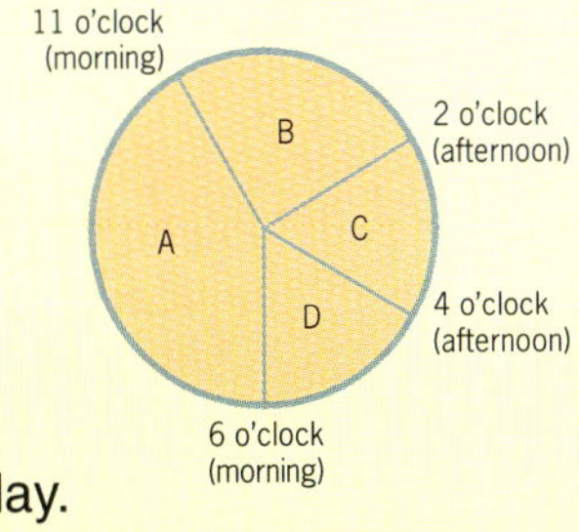

■ – the hottest part of the day.
■ – the rain forest starts to become hot.
■ – heavy rain storms with thunder and lightning.
■ – the storm begins to die out.

Activity E

Copy and complete the following passage, using the words in the box to help you.

There is heavy __________ rainfall most days in the rain forest of __________ . In the morning the __________ gets very hot. This heats the air near the ground, and the air starts to __________ . As the air rises it cools and __________ form. There is a heavy storm in the __________ .

afternoon	Brazil	convection
land	rise	clouds

Activity F

Look at Photograph 1. Write five sentences or more about what it is like in the rain forest in the afternoon.

The Geography of Brazil

- What do we need to know about the geography of a country?

Let's take a look at Brazil.

This section is about asking questions in geography.

To find out about the geography of a place you must learn to ask questions.

One of the most important questions to ask about the geography of a country is **'where is it?'**

Look at Figure 1. It shows the location of Brazil.

Another important question is **'what is it like there?'**

Figure 2 shows some sentences about Brazil. Some of them show that Brazil is the same as many other countries. But some of them show that Brazil is different to other countries.

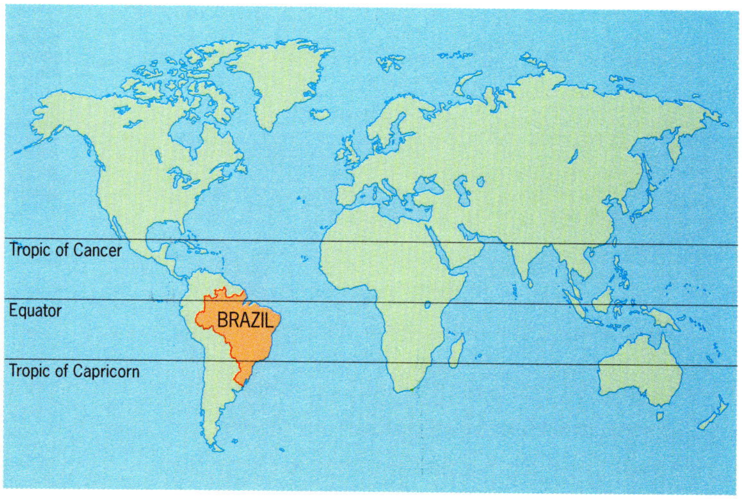

Figure 1

How do you choose which sentences are most important?

LOOK! Read the sentences carefully.
THINK! Do the sentences tell you if Brazil is the same or different?
CHOOSE! If it is different, then it usually means it is important.
WRITE! Make it clear.

This is the beginning of asking questions in geography. To understand the geography of a country, we need to understand what makes it different.

BRAZIL

- Brazil is a country in the continent of South America.
- Brazil is the fifth largest country in the world.
- Brazil is a hot country, and nearly all of it lies in the tropics.
- Brazil has the largest area of rain forest in the world.
- Brazil is a developing country and has many natural resources.
- Brazil's biggest cities are São Paulo, Rio de Janeiro, Belo Horizonte and Salvador.
- Brazil grows more coffee beans than any other country.
- Brazil has more water for HEP than any other country.
- Brazil's regions are all different.
- Brazil owes large amounts of money to other countries.

Figure 2

Activity A

Look at the sentences about Brazil (Figure 2).

1 Choose the sentences that show Brazil is the same as many other countries. Copy them.
2 Choose the sentences that show Brazil is different to many other countries. Copy them.

Activity B

Look again at the sentences that show Brazil is different. Write them down again, and put them in the order that **you** think is important.

Look at these photographs of Brazil.

Photograph 1 Brazil grows more coffee beans than any other country in the world

Photograph 2 Football is the most popular sport in Brazil

Photograph 3 Brazil is the home of the world's largest rain forest

Photograph 4 Brazil has rich parts and poor parts

Photograph 5 Many people in Brazil live in favelas in the big cities

Activity C

Look at the photographs and write a sentence about each one.

Answer like this: **Photograph 1 shows …**

Activity D

Match these key words with their meanings below.

Answer like this: **Rural means in the countryside.**

Rural	Urban	Manufacture	Favela
Wealth	Leisure	Resources	Scale

- ____________ means how rich a country is.
- ____________ means how big something is.
- ____________ means making things.
- ____________ means a slum.
- ____________ means in the countryside.
- ____________ means in the towns and cities.
- ____________ means what there is to work with.
- ____________ means to have fun.

Activity E

1 Write down a sentence about each of the photographs, so there is a key word from Activity E in each of your sentences.

2 Choose your three most important sentences and write them down in the order you think is the most important.

The Development of a Country

- The world is always changing.

Where are the rich and poor countries?

This section is about asking more questions in geography.

In geography the question 'what is a country like?' may mean one of two things.

1 'What is the physical geography like?' This asks about the natural environment, such as the rivers, the mountains, the climate and the weather.

2 'What is the human geography like?' This asks about the people, such as where they live and how they live.

The way a country develops is an important part of its human geography.

This map shows the rich countries, the poor countries, and the developing countries.

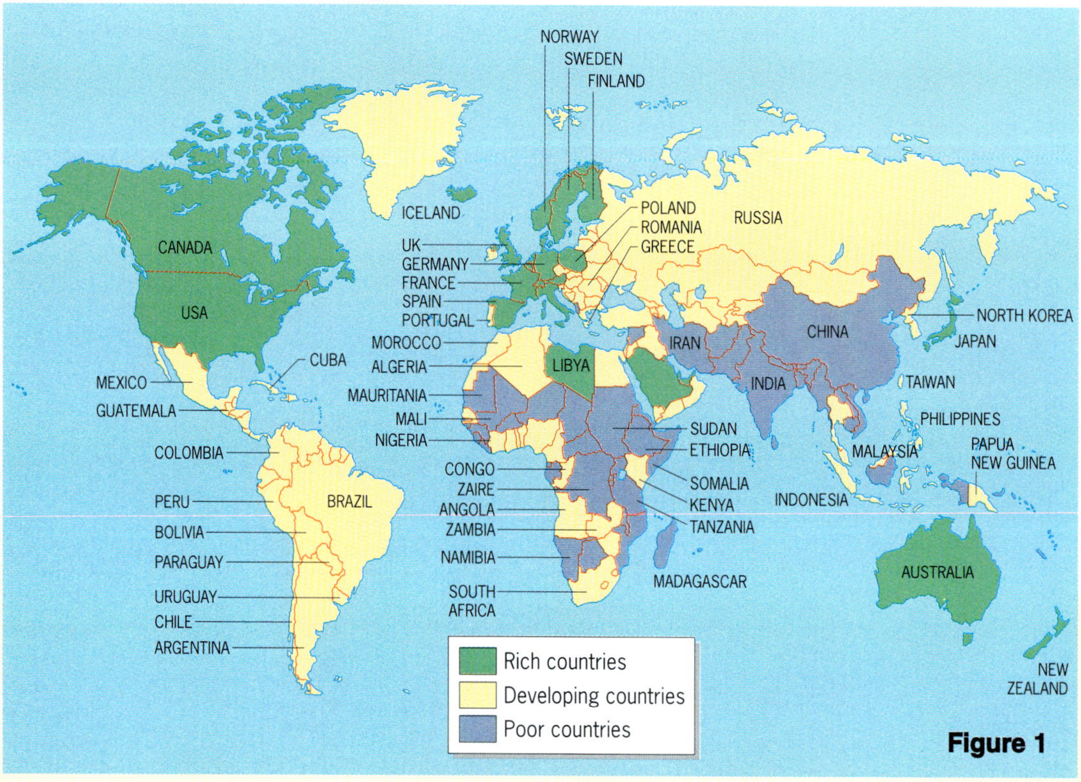

Figure 1

Activity A

Copy and complete these sentences.

1. Physical geography is about the (environment / people).
2. Human geography is about the (environment / people).

Activity B

Look at Figure 1.

1. Name five rich countries.
2. Name five poor countries.
3. Name five developing countries.

Activity C

Look at Figure 1.

1. Name five countries that are as rich as the UK.
2. Name five countries that are not as rich as the UK.

Activity D

1. Name the continent with the most rich countries.
2. Name the continent with the most poor countries.

As a country develops, the way of life improves for its people. A developing country has areas that are more developed than others. Look at these drawings:

Figure 2

Activity E

Look at Figure 2, and copy and complete these sentences.

1 Drawings A and B show (education / health / farming).

2 Drawings C and D show (education / health / farming).

3 Drawings E and F show (education / health / farming).

Activity F

1 Write a sentence about each drawing, and include a key word in each sentence.

2 Write down your six key words.

Activity G

1 Write two sentences to show how the education in the country has developed.

2 Write two sentences to show how the farming in the country has developed.

3 Write two sentences to show how health has developed in the country.

Activity H

Write a sentence about each of the following to explain how you think they will change as a country develops.

1 Road transport

2 Rail transport

3 Houses

4 Entertainment

Development in Brazil and Italy

- All countries have rich and poor people.

Look at Italy and Brazil.

This section is about differences in the same country.

Words that help to explain anything that is difficult are called **key words**. Sentences with key words in them are **key sentences**.

When a number of key sentences tell us the most important things about a place, they are called a **summary**.

Look at these photographs.

Photograph 1

Like all countries in Western Europe, Italy is a developed country. But this photograph of Italy does not look much like a developed country.

Photograph 2

Like most of the countries in South America, Brazil is a developing country. But this photograph of an area in the rain forest looks more like a developed country.

Activity A

Look at these words about Photograph 1.

washing	slum	street	narrow
untidy	poor	run-down	signs
steps	car	old	

1 Copy the words that you think are key words.
2 Write five key sentences about Photograph 1.

Activity B

1 Write down three key words about Photograph 2.
2 Write three key sentences about Photograph 2.

Activity C

1 How does Photograph 1 show that this part of Italy is less developed?
2 How does Photograph 2 show that this part of Brazil is developed?

Photograph 3 shows farming in a part of Italy. Italy is a developed country, but it has regions that are less developed.

Photograph 4 shows farming in a part of Brazil. Brazil is a developing country. Some parts of Brazil are developed, while other parts are less developed.

Photograph 3

Photograph 4

Activity D

Look at these words about Photograph 3. Copy the words that you think are key words.

flat	house	tree	regular	vines
sky	road	fertile	daytime	rich

Activity E

Look at Photograph 4. Write down five key words to say what the photograph shows about development.

Activity F

Write six key sentences about the development shown in Photograph 3.

Activity G

Match the summaries below with the photographs.

Photograph 1	Photograph 2
Photograph 3	Photograph 4

- ________________ is a developing part of Brazil. It is a farming area where many people work in the fields. There are very few machines, and most of the work is done by hand.
- ________________ is a poor city in Italy. The streets are narrow and dirty, with few cars. It is not well looked after.
- ________________ is a city in the rain forest of Brazil. The buildings are big and well looked after. It is a clean and modern city.
- ________________ is a developed farming area in the North of Italy. The fields are big and flat and the crops are grown close together on the rich soil. The farm houses are modern.

Activity H

1 Write a summary about how a photograph can show a place is less developed.

2 Write a summary about how a photograph can show a place is developed.

The Development of the UK

- What do you need to know about your own country?

Let's see how the UK is changing.

This section is about development in the UK.

The UK is a developed country. But there are parts of the UK that are more developed than others.

In a developed country like the UK there are many modern **service** industries.

These photographs show some of the things used in service industries in the UK today.

The photographs show how **information and communication technology (ICT)** is used to help service industries to develop.

Some developed countries have better ICT than others. The USA and Japan use a lot of this technology.

In a developing country, some parts may not have this technology.

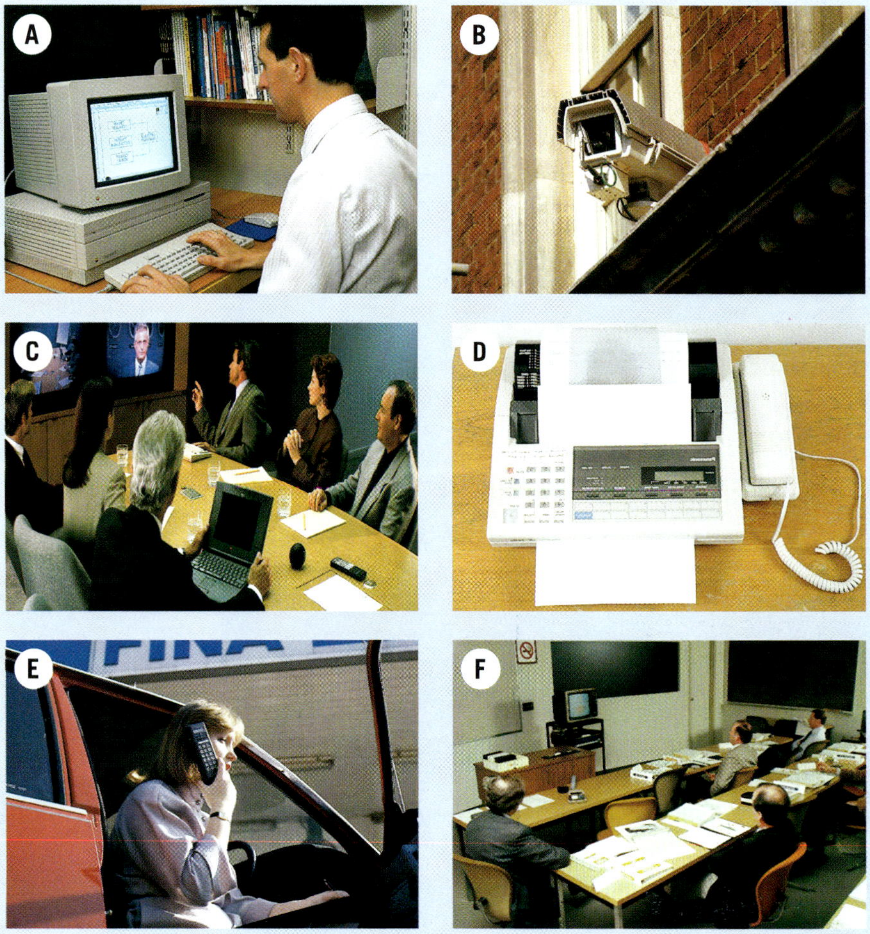

Figure 1

Activity A

Match the photographs in Figure 1 with the ICT below.

mobile phone	computer
camera	fax
video conferencing	television

Activity B

Name five jobs that use each of the following:

1 A telephone
2 A computer
3 A camera

Activity C

Write down ten jobs in the service industry.

Activity D

Look at Figure 1 and write down how each of the things you can see is used in any service industry.

Activity E

1 Look at Figure 1 and choose three things you think could help a developing country.
2 Write a sentence about how each one could help a country to develop.

The UK is a country that has developed by selling and buying goods with other countries. This is called **trade**. There are many **service industries** needed when countries trade. This includes industries like transport, banking and insurance.

The UK also makes many things in factories. This is called **manufacturing** and the things made in factories are called **products**. Some manufacturing industries in the UK make large products like cars, ships and steel. This is called **heavy manufacturing**. There are also many factories in the UK making smaller products like cameras, televisions and washing machines. These are products that we use every day. This is called **light manufacturing**.

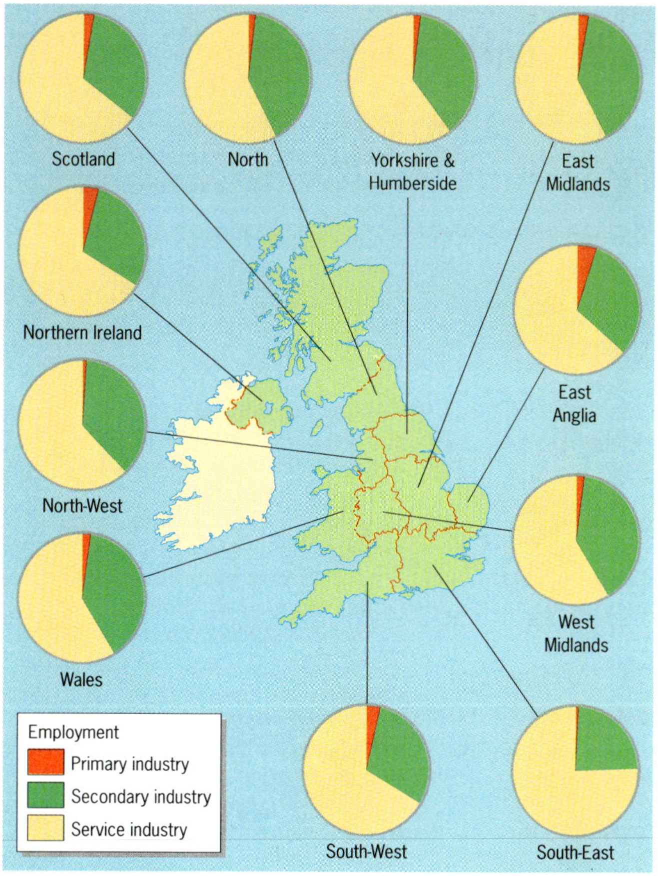

Figure 2

Manufacturing makes up the group of industries called **secondary industry**. In a less developed country there may be very little manufacturing and the services will not be very good.

In a developing country like Brazil there may be a great deal of trade with other countries, but not much manufacturing. Brazil has less manufacturing than the UK.

Most of the heavy manufacturing industries in the UK started on or near to the coalfields.

Many of the service industries, like shops and offices, are in the centre of towns and cities. In the UK today there are more and more service industries moving out of city centres to places where there is more space.

There are also many more light industries than there used to be in the UK. The new factories are located in places where there are good roads. This makes it easy to bring in the parts and send out the products. Industry is always changing.

Activity F

Copy and complete the sentences below.

1 Buying and selling with other countries is called (manufacturing / trade).
2 Things made in factories are called (products / services).
3 Making cars is called (heavy / light) manufacturing.
4 Making cameras is called (heavy / light) manufacturing.

Activity G

Copy and complete this chart to classify these products.

Cars	Ships	Cameras
Washing machines	Steel making	Televisions
Chemical products	Watches	

Heavy manufacturing	Light manufacturing
Cars	

Activity H

1 Look at Figure 2 and name the region with the most workers in service industry.
2 Name the region with the most workers in primary industry.

Index and Glossary

active	*page 19*	Another word for alive.
agriculture	*28*	Another word for farming.
alphabetical	*16*	The same order as letters of the alphabet.
altitude	*62*	The height of the land.
anticline	*60*	Layers of rock that are folded up.
arable	*38*	Food crops, like wheat, barley and oats.
aspect	*61*	The direction of the slope of the land.
atlas	*16*	A book of maps.
buttress	*31*	A prop used to keep something standing up straight.
canopy	*31*	A cover of leaves in the forest.
citrus	*69*	A type of fruit, e.g. oranges, lemons, limes and grapefruits.
climate	*65*	The average weather over a long period of time.
climograph	*68*	A graph showing the climate of a place.
commercial	*28*	Something done for money.
compete	*31*	To try hard against others.
contrasts	*23*	When different things are next to each other.
contour	*56*	A line on a map joining places of the same height.
data	*64*	The information needed, e.g. to draw a graph.
degrees	*14*	Units of measurement for latitude and longitude.
dormant	*19*	Another word for sleeping.
drought	*69*	A long period without rain.
earthquake	*20*	A shaking of the land.
ecosystem	*11*	An area where there is a balance between the animals, plants and climate.
emigration	*63*	Moving from one country to another.
environment	*11*	The world around us.
equator	*8*	A line on a map drawn around the middle of the Earth.
erosion	*25*	When something is worn away.
eruption	*18*	When magma breaks out on to the Earth's surface.
extinct	*19*	Another word for dead.
fault	*18*	A crack in the Earth's crust.
favela	*23*	Poor houses or slums in Brazil.
fazenda	*40*	A very large farm in Brazil.
fodder	*38*	Food for animals.
hydro-electric power	*47*	Electricity made by the power of falling water. Also called HEP for short.
immigrant	*63*	A person who goes to live in another country.
index	*16*	A list of places in an atlas.
irrigation	*69*	Using springs and rivers to water the land.
key words	*76*	Important words.
lava	*18*	Molten rock on the surface of the Earth.
lianas	*31*	Creeping plants.
magma	*18*	Molten rock deep inside the Earth.
maquis	*12*	Vegetation in Mediterranean countries.
market garden	*38*	A farm that grows vegetables, flowers and fruit.
maximum	*67*	The most of something.
Mezzogiorno	*12*	The South of Italy.
migrant	*63*	A person who goes to live in another part of the country.
minimum	*67*	The lowest of something.
molten	*18*	When something is so hot that it melts.
hemisphere	*8*	One half of the world.
humid	*24*	Hot and wet.
latitude	*14*	Lines running across maps in an atlas.
longitude	*14*	Lines running up and down maps in an atlas.
manufacturing	*79*	Making things in factories.
plantation	*40*	A very large farm.
population	*63*	The people of a place.
port	*54*	A type of settlement where the river meets the sea.
rain gauge	*65*	A weather instrument used to measure rainfall.
rain shadow	*59*	The side of a hill or mountain that has less rain.
range	*67*	The difference between the maximum and minimum.
relief	*53*	The shape of the land.
rural depopulation	*63*	The movement of people from the countryside to the cities.
scale	*44*	The link between shape and size.
section	*57*	A flat surface made by cutting through a solid, like a side view.
sedimentary	*60*	Laid down in water, like a sea or lake.
selvas	*24*	The rain forest in Brazil.
service	*78*	A job where people serve others.
shifting cultivation	*40*	A type of faming in the rain forest.
site	*54*	The place where a settlement starts to grow.
source	*61*	Where a river starts.
squatters	*23*	People who live in favelas.
strata	*60*	Layers of rock.
subsistence	*28*	The lowest amount of food needed to support life.
summary	*76*	A number of key sentences.
syncline	*60*	The low parts of folded rock.
temperate	*7*	Not very hot or very cold.
terraces	*20*	Large steps cut into the sides of hills and mountains.
thermometer	*67*	A weather instrument used to measure heat.
tourists	*17*	People on holiday.
trade	*79*	Selling and buying goods with other people
tropic	*8*	Area of the world that is hot all year round.
undergrowth	*32*	Small plants.
urbanisation	*23*	The way towns and cities grow.
vegetation	*11*	Plants and trees.
vineyard	*19*	A farm that grows grapes to make wine.
volcano	*18*	A type of mountain.
weather	*65*	The day-to-day changes in temperature, rainfall and the air.